Diana J. Sweeney
Brooklyn 1964

TRAVEL

BOLIVIA '57-'59

THE STARS WEEP

San Benito, patron saint of Aymara Negroes

BERNARD LELONG
AND JEAN-LUC JAVAL

THE STARS WEEP

Translated from the French by
GEOFFREY SAINSBURY

With 36 Illustrations

LONDON · HUTCHINSON

Hutchinson & Co. (Publishers) Ltd.
178–202 Great Portland Street, London, W.1

London   Melbourne   Sydney   Auckland
Bombay Johannesburg New York Toronto

First published in English 1956

A version of this book has also been
published in French under the title
Cordillère Magique
(Amiot-Dumont)

Printed in Great Britain
by The Anchor Press, Ltd.,
Tiptree, Essex

For the sake of clarity for the reader we have let Bernard speak the narrative in this book, but materially we wrote it together as our joint work.

JEAN-LUC JAVAL.
BERNARD LELONG.

CONTENTS

LIST OF ILLUSTRATIONS

PROLOGUE

WHICH of us was it that stumbled on Rouma's work on the Aymaras and Quechuas of Bolivia and Peru? Was it Jean-Luc or myself? Never mind which; what matters is that some pages of this Belgian ethnologist's work, picked up on the shelves of the Musée de l'Homme, dealt with the organization of village communities whose origins run far back into the past and which the Inca rulers respected and fostered throughout the length and breadth of their domains.

Then came the Conquistadors. They tried to stamp out this social organization which ran counter to Spanish ideas and traditions, but they never succeeded.

The War of Liberation. The names of its heroes, San Martin, Bolivar, floated on the winds of the Andes right down to the Argentine Pampas. The new Republics of South America were born. But what had been there since the beginning of time remained unshaken, the ancestral village communities.

A century passed. Rouma's book appeared. What did he say of these communities? Not much, indeed; but he does tell us that in 1924 and 1925, on the high plateaux of Bolivia and Peru, Indians were still leading a communal existence, working collectively under the direction of their chiefs. The chiefs, elected for a year, were called *ilacatas* in some parts, *curacas* in others. They carried a baton ringed with silver, and a cross hung on their chests. It seemed also that the community was ritually divided into two rival parts.

Looking for further details on this subject, which had somehow got under our skins, we found them sadly lacking.

We were in touch with all the ethnologists in Paris. Professor Rivet advised us not to confine our attention to the highlands but to push on to the forests of the Amazon basin in the North, where two tribes existed, the Cholones and the Jibitos, about which practically nothing at all was known.

We liked the idea, which would take us to the climatic extremes of Indian civilization, from the cold and arid Altiplano 13,000 feet above sea level to the dense, low-lying, tropical forest. What should we find in common between these people living under such utterly different conditions?

We wished to go as a properly accredited mission. Months passed, then more months, and our projected journey came to be treated by everyone as a joke. But we didn't give up. Jean-Luc went on with his studies in Paris, while I endeavoured to perfect my Spanish in Madrid. Things had come to look very black indeed when one fine morning I received a letter from Jean-Luc telling me we would be leaving at the end of April.

It was with very wide terms of reference that the C.N.R.S. (Centre National de la Recherche Scientifique) instructed us to proceed. The whole field was thrown open to us, and we were to wander through vast tracts of country. We knew that the shades of the Incas would follow us everywhere: we should have them with us in the ruins of Tiahuanaco as well as in those of Cuzco and Machu-Pichu, we should find them by Copacabana on the 'royal road' which runs down to Lake Titicaca.

When we finally set out, it was after delays of over a year and a half. By this time we knew each other well, well enough to be sure that our friendship would stand up to whatever trials were in store for us. We had much in common, and our differences never estranged us. Our friends never ceased to warn us that an enterprise such as ours would put any friendship to the test. That it certainly did, but the friendship came through unscathed.

It was on May 10th, 1953, that we embarked on the *Alain Louis Dreyfus* at Dunkirk.

Dakar, Santos, Rio de Janeiro, Buenos Aires. Then the train to La Paz. For five days it crossed the Pampas, the Gran Chaco, then climbed up into the Andes and rumbled over the Altiplano.

It is the story of our travels which is related here. The more scientific side of our researches will be published elsewhere.

I

The Altiplano

WE had hardly had time to get acclimatized to Bolivia when we were already on our way from La Paz to Jesus de Machaca, where we were to study our first Indian communities.

We drove in a green jeep lent by the Inter-American Education Service and we had with us two Bolivians—a guide and an interpreter.

Fernando Aramayo, who held a high post in the Ministry of National Education, had been placed at our disposal by the Bolivian Government, and we were going to find him not only the most helpful collaborator, but an ideal travelling companion. A short, swarthy man about forty, who spoke French, he never failed to keep us amused. Moreover, he knew his country and the Aymara language.

The other, who drove the jeep, was Marcelino Velasquez, but that wasn't the name we knew him by. Like every other grown-up man-servant in Bolivia, he was known as the Macho, which simply means the male. Massively built, he had pronounced Indian features, and it was easy to see that, despite his gloriously Andalusian name, the blood in his veins was much less Spanish than Aymara.

Aramayo and the Macho rendered valuable service and we owe much to their devotion.

. . . . . .

Our track struck right across the Altiplano. An evocative name that, and we had often tried to imagine this high desert plateau, stronghold of ancient Indian traditions.

A vast plain, stretching endlessly on every side. So widely separated were the villages that often we could see nothing but the dusty track ahead till it disappeared among the endless tufts of yellowish grass.

Two motionless companions reared their heads over the horizon, Ilimani and Illampu, sacred mountains of the Indians, seats of the gods, which the advance of Christianity had not yet robbed of their power. Even at La Paz, the Indians follow their sorcerers up onto the surrounding hills at noon or midnight several times a week to make offerings of drink to the spirit of Ilimani.

13

The dry crisp air chaps hands and lips. The newcomer from Europe soon finds his skin has gone rough and taken on the coppery hue of the natives, and when he returns to La Paz everyone comments on it.

The dryness is quite extraordinary. The rains are confined to the summer months—December, January and February—and even then the water quickly disappears to join the water-bearing seam ten feet below the surface, though the occasional windmill suffices to show that, with the wind that blows all the year round, it would be an easy matter to irrigate the whole of this region whose soil is dusty but potentially fertile.

Monotonous though it was, we didn't complain of the flatness, which made walking easy. With the rarity of the air, the slightest gradient meant a painful effort. Europeans have not the chest development of the Indians and they are often afflicted by the ills of high altitude which are called *puna* and *sorache*.

We had been driving for an hour when two red stone towers appeared over the horizon, belonging, as Aramayo told us, to the church of Laja, the oldest perhaps in the whole of Bolivia, older certainly than the founding of La Paz.

We stopped to look at it. The two red towers stood up against the invariably blue sky of the Altiplano. A wonderful nave. The dome, which had from outside seemed rather squat, was a marvel of lightness when viewed from the interior. The hard light of the Altiplano charged with ultra-violet rays was subdued by four windows of diaphanous alabaster to a gentle radiance.

The altar was completely encased with chased silver and the retable was of the same metal. The baroque statues would have been worthy of a place in the museum of Valladolid.

Squatting like a tailor in front of the altar to the Virgin, her hat put down in front of her, an Indian woman was muttering prayers.

"Why has she removed her hat?" we asked Aramayo.

"They always do, perhaps because the women's hats in the Paz region are so like the white man's bowler."

Completely absorbed, she gazed at the statue of the Virgin, stretched out imploring hands, and wept. Sometimes she stopped praying as though expecting an answer. Then she would start again, her voice rising to a plaintive wail, but so inarticulate that Aramayo was quite unable to distinguish the words.

We got back to the jeep, where the Macho was waiting for us.

"That church was built by the Incas," he said.

Quite an erroneous belief, but one firmly rooted in the popular mind. Perhaps there had been a sanctuary here in the days of the Incas. The famous Spanish chronicler, Pedro Cieza de León, mentions Laja as a stopping place on the way to La Paz a little to one side of the 'royal road of the Incas'.

We drove on. From Laja to Tiahuanaco the track stretched drearily across the plain. Occasionally, as we gazed ahead, we would see a lorryload of Indians in multi-coloured headgear, throwing up behind them a huge cloud of dust.

At the entrance to Tiahuanaco stand the ruins of the famous sanctuary. The beautiful Gate of the Sun faces west to catch the last rays of sunset. Its surface is carved all over with mythological scenes, which, however, are quite unintelligible, as they depict the religion and cosmogony of a people who lived here long before the Incas. A little further on stands a monolith which has been nicknamed The Monk. But alas, of the sanctuary itself, nothing remains but a few rows of dressed stones and the base of a gigantic staircase. Some excavations have been done, but with the abominable methods of the nineteenth century. Most of what was found was taken to Berlin, the little that was left being deposited in a square in La Paz. Since then there has been no methodical excavation, and you have only to bend down to pick up bits of pottery and small copper objects, pins, spoons, etc.

Having inspected the ruins, we settled down to have our midday meal near the Gate of the Sun. Our improvised table we called the Incas' dining-room.

We were all in high spirits. Before long we were surrounded by Indian children who offered us stone ornaments they had carved with their knives.

They asked absurdly little for them, but even so Aramayo told us we must bargain. I love nothing better than an argument and was quite ready to, but first of all I sent the children off to look for any copper objects they could pick up.

Over a wall near the railway line floated two Bolivian flags and a white one. We asked why.

"There must be a wedding on," Aramayo told us.

This was confirmed by the old soldier who guarded the ruins. Putting off my bargaining till later, I asked if we could witness it.

"Of course."

We went off at once as fast as we could. We didn't want to miss anything. We couldn't run, on account of the rarity of the air, but it became something of a walking race, and our skins were itching when we arrived.

"Why didn't you wait for the Macho?" asked Aramayo, when he caught up with us. "He went to fetch the jeep. Here he is, so you haven't gained anything by your hurry."

We didn't bother about that, as we were already listening intently to the music that was being played. We soon recovered our breath, and the itching ceased.

The drum dominated. The tempo was rapid, the rhythm strongly marked. It stopped, and the sound of a flute floated over the wall of the little courtyard in front of the house.

"Do you hear the *kéna*?" asked Aramayo.

"Is that what you call it, that flute?"

"Yes."

We stood just outside the mud wall which shut us off from the scene within. On our left was a small arched doorway, through which Indians dressed in their *ponchos* kept coming and going.

They came out to speak to a man who was holding three mules and a horse, all harnessed. Having said something to him they went back into the yard. We should have liked to follow them, but didn't quite dare. Standing in a little group close to the doorway and peering in, we tried to see what was going on. All we could make out was a crowd of Indians moving to and fro.

Suddenly the music stopped. A member of the family came out and started talking to Aramayo in Aymara. The conversation went on a long time. Our guide seemed to be negotiating. We guessed he was being asked what we were doing there and very likely requested to take us away.

Finally Aramayo turned to us.

"He's asking what you've come for. I've told him you're studying the customs of the country. He says he's very pleased and invites you to come inside. Come on. It's all right."

We didn't wait to be asked twice.

The Indians didn't appear to be in the least embarrassed by our presence, nor even by Jean-Luc's camera, though each time he attempted to take one of the gaunt-faced old Indians the latter would give him a baleful look and run into the house for cover. Their fierce eyes were impressive enough and we did not care to insist, lest their ill humour spread to the remainder of the company.

Bernard Lelong, Le Macho, and Aramayo. A picnic on the Altiplano

The Corregidor at Jesus de Machaca

All the men round us wore white *ponchos*, made of an enormous piece of stuff with a hole in the middle for the head to go through. The *poncho* falls rather low in front and behind and somewhat resembles the flowing old-style chasubles worn by Catholic priests. Even at the sides it falls low enough to hide a man's hands if he stands like a soldier at attention.

"What do you call that cap the men wear?"

"A *llucho*."

It is made of knitted wool and has ear-flaps from the ends of which a pompom dangles on a string. Most *lluchos* are brightly coloured, sometimes plain, sometimes patterned, either geometrically or with highly stylized llamas, suns, etc.

The *llucho* and the *poncho* effectively keep out the bitter cold of the Altiplano, particularly at dawn and dusk.

The women, who are less in the open than the men, are wrapped in voluminous black shawls. They wear the classic hard hat, like a bowler, black, grey, or chestnut in the region of La Paz.

Not all the *ponchos* were white, however, nor all the shawls black. Soon a highly-coloured quartet came forward, two men in vermilion *ponchos*, the women in shawls of the same colour and many superimposed multicoloured skirts or petticoats.

"Who are they?"

"The bride and her godmother, the bridegroom and his godfather."

They formed up in a line between the two flagstaffs with the Bolivian flags. The white flag, whose staff was stuck into the caked mud wall, hung down exactly over the bride's head.

"Why do they wear red?"

"It's the proper thing for a wedding," answered Aramayo.

The guests filed past. Friends and relations congratulated the young couple, who stood quite still and silent. The bridegroom's mouth was concealed by a scarf which he was certainly not wearing for warmth. The godparents, on the other hand, were most lively, particularly the godfather, who had something to say to everyone. His hand was constantly diving under his *poncho* to pull out a bottle of spirits, a tot of which he would pour into a little glass and hand to one of the guests.

Sometimes a guest would produce a bottle too and offer it freely round.

A boy in a soft felt hat much too big for him was going from

B

group to group. As he passed, an Indian would fold a banknote diagonally and tuck it into the hat-ribbon. We did the same. Before long the coloured notes formed a crown reminiscent of a Red Indian's feathers.

"What's the money for?" asked Jean-Luc.

"To buy more drink," said the Macho.

The faces of the bridal couple wore an expression of sadness like the resignation of slaves. But that was only a first impression.

The godfather beckoned to us and we each had a glass of spirits. It was horrible sour stuff with a nasty taste of distillation. Bits of leaves floated in it.

"What leaf is it?"

"Coca."

"They put coca in their spirits?"

"Oh no. They chew it. But sometimes they have such a lot in their mouths that they leave some behind in the glass. Look at that one over there. His mouth's so full of coca leaves that his lips are quite green."

These festivities gave us an opportunity of observing how the Indians make use of coca. From time to time they pull out a leaf or two from a rectangular bag and put them in their mouths. The resulting quid may be as big as a pigeon's egg. To precipitate the cocaine (an alkaloid) a base is necessary, so they chew at the same time lime mixed with ashes.

Of course we had to try for ourselves, but we could find nothing pleasant in the acrid leaves which made our tongues and gums smart. Later we learned that the Indians, who make an inveterate habit of it, sometimes have their tongues badly inflamed.

Delighted though we were to have got inside the courtyard, we were at a loss to understand what was going on. Were the bride and bridegroom already married? Had they just returned from the church? Prompted by us, Aramayo made inquiries.

"What we see here," he explained, "is the last part of the festivities. This is the house of the bride's parents. Yesterday, after the ceremony in church, celebrations were held at the bridegroom's home. Presently the married couple and the godparents will ride off on the mounts you saw outside to the young people's new home, where the marriage will be consummated."

"And the parents . . ." I began.

I broke off, as an Indian on the doorstep was making friendly signs to me. Going in, I saw a large oval table at which sat men and women. In the middle of one side sat an old man, presiding, with women on either side of him. Other Indians came and went, squatting for a while, tailor-fashion, round the room, drinking and talking.

The furnishings were rudimentary. The table, a few benches, and on the walls some sheepskins and llama skins.

The old man offered me a glass of spirits which I couldn't refuse, much as I would have liked to. And being indoors, I was unable to follow the advice Aramayo had given us—to keep the stuff in our mouths, and then spit it out when no one was looking. Like a wine-taster.

I sat down in a corner beside an Indian who spoke a little Spanish.

"Who's the old man at the table?"

"The bridegroom's father."

"And the women on either side of him?"

"The mother, aunts, and sisters."

"And the others at the table?"

"Relations."

"And the bride's family?"

"They're in another building. The best place is kept for the bridegroom's people."

And sure enough, as I came away, I caught sight of them squatting on the ground in an outhouse to which they seemed to have been banished.

Presently we were invited to eat. Each guest, holding out a corner of his *poncho*, went up to the bridegroom's father who dropped on it a few handfuls of *chuños* and some boiled maize. The *chuño* is a potato which has been frozen and trampled on to squeeze out the water. Shrunk to a withered grey ball, it tastes rather like a boiled chestnut.

The eating over, dancing began. Everyone danced, old and young alike, forming up in quadrilles, then re-forming. The music never stopped, and no one ever seemed to get tired.

Indoors an interminable discussion was going on concerning the departure of the young couple. It couldn't take place till the bridegroom's father had given the word, and the old man couldn't make up his mind to do so.

We wished he would. We had intended to reach Jesus de Machaca before nightfall, but we didn't want to leave till we had witnessed the end.

A stir. The two families emerged into the courtyard. The young couple with their godparents went out to the horse and mules. Many of the guests walked across a field to where a track led away. I went ahead with the group that was leaving. Jean-Luc lagged behind with Aramayo, filming the proceedings. Part of the bridegroom's family who had remained near the house emitted shrill cries in Aymara.

Arriving at the end of the field, the bride squatted down and the next moment her godmother followed suit. They got up again. I hadn't understood the shouting and imagined they had been gratifying the calls of nature. Aramayo, rejoining the group, who were now mounting, translated the shouts.

"The godfather is a rotter: he has forgotten to make the bride pee. Make her pee, idiot, otherwise he won't be able."

Jean-Luc was so shaken with laughter that he was afraid he had jolted his camera.

Three of the four rode astride. Only the bride sat cross-legged on top of a bundle that had been thrown across the saddle and contained her dowry.

They made off rapidly along the track, escorted for a while by some of the guests who, however, soon came back to the house, where the dancing had started again.

We said good-bye to the couple's parents, though they pressed us to stay till the evening. When we got back to the Gate of the Sun we found the children again who looked at us craftily. The ones we had tried to beat down still held to their prices.

When one of them came up to me, I forestalled him with:

"I told you I wanted things of copper."

"I've got one at home."

"What is it?"

"My father found it digging the foundations of a house."

"Go and fetch it."

The boy was soon back, walking as quickly as he could under what was obviously a heavy load.

It was a hexagonal block weighing some thirty pounds. The price was not exorbitant and after very little haggling the deal was clenched. Jean-Luc protested:

"You're not going to encumber yourself with that lump, are you? You don't even know if it's a genuine antiquity. It's certainly not an object of beauty."

"It's a bargain," I said firmly, stowing away the object, which was soon forgotten, except from time to time when I was twitted about my acquisition.

The jeep started off and we drove through the village of Tiahuanaco, most of whose houses were built of stones filched from the ruins.

We were soon within sight of Guaqui on the shore of Lake Titicaca big as an inland sea. There was something magical about its blue water which we stood gazing at in admiration. According to Cieza de León, Guaqui was founded by the Incas who maintained a garrison there.

Night was falling when we got through the customs barrier. We refused courteous invitations to stay, and pushed on again. The road began to climb. In the glare of our headlamps the mountain scenery was like a landscape in the moon. The road was bad, frequently traversed by streams which had to be forded. Often we had to stop to roll aside big stones, which the Indians place in the evenings to prevent cars using the roads. It meant keeping a sharp look-out, for the stones were often placed at turnings, where they constituted a grave danger.

We soon realized we should arrive at Jesus de Machaca too late to find a suitable place at which to put up, so Aramayo decided we had best stop at a *finca*, that is to say a farm, whose proprietor was a friend of his.

We lost our way in the darkness several times. Aramayo assured us that the farm we were looking for, the Finca Corpa, should be on the left and visible from the road. Now and again the Macho turned the car to sweep the countryside with his headlamps. If we came across an Indian, we called out to him but he promptly made off to hide in the bushes. Finally the lamps lit up a bit of white wall which Aramayo recognized as the chapel belonging to the *finca*.

We found the farm shut up. In the sharp dry cold of the night, the stars shone with absolute purity. We had all got out of the jeep, and we walked up and down to keep warm. Aramayo shouted for the caretaker. He was a long time coming. Finally he appeared.

"Call Señor Lupe. Tell him Señor Aramayo's here."

"Señor Lupe is away. He went to La Paz today."

Aramayo had been to the place before, and in the end the caretaker recognized him. There was a long discussion about sleeping quarters for us. Finally we were all taken to a mud hut in which a whole Indian family was already installed.

"I can't open Señor Lupe's house," said the caretaker. "I haven't the keys.

The mud hut was certainly uninviting. The doorway was the only opening, doing duty at the same time as window and chimney, and it was so low that we had to bend double to get through. The earthen stove gave off acrid fumes which stung our eyes and throats. Having got more or less used to this, we found beneath it that strong human smell that Europeans find so difficult to bear.

"Delightful," said Jean-Luc ironically. "I think I'll sleep beautifully here."

We wondered what to do. I thought of the chapel and asked if the Indians had the key of that. They had.

"Why shouldn't we put our camp-beds there? Let's go and see."

We trooped out, and a moment later, like the Big Four, we were parcelling out the chapel into zones of influence.

"I'll take the chapel of the Virgin," said one of us.

At that point, the caretaker announced that he had found the key of his employer's kitchen.

That was obviously a much better solution. We were soon settling in there, while Aramayo mixed a lemon *pisco*. *Pisco* is a sort of brandy, and very good, too. A drink did us a lot of good, but made us very hungry and, with that, more than ever conscious of the cold.

The kitchen was almost luxurious and amply big enough to hold our four camp-beds in addition to its own furniture. First of all the stove had to be lit. The Indian and I saw to that. He began with some dried grasses which flared up in a second. To the flames he cautiously added withered branches he called *tola*, which looked rather like heather. In a receptacle near the stove I found some small grey things which I took, in the half-light, for olives. I was on the point of putting one in my mouth when Aramayo snatched my hand away.

"You're not going to start eating llama's dung, I hope!"

And he added:

"It's food for the fire, not for you."

And excellent fuel it was.

We hurried through our meal and then turned in, under the eyes of the five or six Indians who had come in with us and who spent the whole night watching us sleep, talking incessantly in a low murmur. The Indians have an amazing capacity for conversation, which they can keep up for hours, their voices hardly rising above a whisper. It is impossible to tell what they talk about, for they stop at once when anyone approaches. No doubt that on this occasion they talked about us. Our arrival must have been a great event, not to be exhausted by six or seven hours' conversation.

Through the open door we could see the starry sky. The moon had risen and lit up everything sharply.

Going to sleep that night, 13,500 feet above sea level, we were conscious of the immensity of the Altiplano all round us. At La Paz, built in a hollow, one forgets the wide stretches. Here, everything fell into its proper place. We didn't feel any ill effects from the altitude, not even Jean-Luc who had been so tired at first that we feared he would be unable to face the journey to Jesus de Machaca.

The Indians droned on. Through the doorway I saw a last shooting star, then went off to sleep.

Next morning we wondered what to do. Having found quarters at Corpa, should we make that our headquarters, or go on to Jesus de Machaca, as originally intended? Aramayo was for our staying where we were.

"We're only five kilometres from Jesus de Machaca, and we've got all these Indians of the *finca* to look after us."

"That's all very well," we answered, "but we've come to study the Indians and we'd be better off right in the middle of them."

We hadn't come to a decision when we settled down to the serious business of making breakfast. The fire was lit, but to get on quicker we tried to warm our coffee with some solid fuel we had brought with us, derived from the American army. The result was pitiful. The coffee simply would not get hot. At first we blamed the fuel, then realized that the fault lay with the air which didn't provide enough oxygen for its proper combustion.

The Indians came and went, pottering about amongst us.

"The altitude doesn't seem to bother them," said one of us.

"Look at their chests."

The Indians are short on the whole, but their chests are developed out of all proportion to the rest.

In the end we decided to move on, returning to Corpa if we failed to find quarters at Jesus de Machaca.

"Do you know what Corpa means in Aymara?" asked Aramayo.

"What?"

"Corpa means to lodge. You see how true it is: it has lodged us. Lodging, of course, meant much more in the old days when everyone moved about on horseback or on foot."

II

The *Ilacata*

"IS the jeep ready, Macho?"

"*Si, señores.*"

"Then off we go!"

It was still early when we arrived at Jesus de Machaca.

From the track coming from Guaqui the first thing one catches sight of is the red stone church tower. For a while the track turns back into the desert, then the whole village appears. Nothing but squat, one-storeyed houses built of adobe, the same colour as the soil of the Altiplano, which is what it is. The thatched roofs melt into the landscape.

As the sun rose, the walls took on a warmer glow. The narrow road wound its way between the houses, then came out suddenly onto a huge square, where stood the church whose tower we had seen. It was built in pure colonial style.

Before we had left La Paz, the Archbishop had given us a letter of introduction to any priests we might meet in Bolivia asking them to give us what assistance they could. The Minister of Education had given us a similar one addressed to the civil and military authorities. Finding a police lieutenant in the square, we presented this one to him.

We exchanged the usual courtesies and he placed himself entirely at our disposal.

First of all, he took us to the priest, the Little Father or *Padrecito*, whose response was somewhat less cordial. He wasn't too happy about the idea of our studying the Indians. The Archbishop's letter, however, did much to reassure him, and he offered us a room in the presbytery, where we could instal our camp-beds.

The day passed in visits to the other inhabitants of the village who spoke Spanish, the *corregidor* and the cantor.

A *corregidor* is the representative of the Government. He does all requisitioning for the army and plays somewhat the same part as our justice of the peace. Since this one was almost always drunk, however, the police lieutenant kept him as far as possible in the background.

In the evening we dined by candlelight, wearing everything we had, because of the cold. With us were the lieutenant and his little

24

four-year-old daughter who never left his side for a moment and the angelic-looking priest, who spoke in a gentle, hesitating voice, like a boy.

"I studied in Italy," he told us. "In fact it's barely a year since I left the seminary at Asti. I've only been here six months."

From his sighs we could guess that his task was far from being an easy one. Sorcery, paganism, and drunkenness were, he said, the chief things he had to contend with.

"Only yesterday," he added, "a mother came fifteen kilometres to see me, carrying her still-born child, begging me to baptize it, insisting even. And don't imagine that a case like that is in any way exceptional."

"And you can be quite sure," put in the lieutenant shyly, "that she got what she wanted in the end. As soon as she got home she'd have found someone to act as godfather, perform the ceremony and give the child a name."

Funerals were a particular problem for the priest.

"As a rule I refuse to take part in the funeral procession from the church to the cemetery. The family's cries of joy or suffering drown my prayers. The bearers are always stopping suddenly to have a drink, dropping the stretcher which carries the body.

"The other day I broke my rule and for a while everything went well—in fact, till we reached the cemetery. Then when I stopped to say some prayers, two drunken Indians leant their heads on my shoulders. When I moved forward to give the benediction they had nothing to support them and fell to the ground behind me."

This young priest told us also that witchcraft remained extremely powerful, the sorcerers still holding sway over the natives' minds, their crude and quite ineffective remedies being generally preferred to proper medical treatment.

A little later, when the priest was out of the room for a few minutes, the lieutenant confided to us:

"Some weeks ago I had a nasty cut on my arm. Nothing would make it heal up, so I went to the sorcerer at Yahuriri. He put a bit of lizard skin on the wound. Look! It was here. You can't see a trace of it."

By the end of the meal the *padrecito* had been completely won over. We separated the best of friends. Happy once again to be enjoying European company, he was now anxious to help us all he could.

We awoke next morning to be greeted by a shaft of sunshine which told us the bitter cold of the night had been banished and that in a corner of the courtyard it would be already almost warm. It was there that we washed and dressed.

We were very sorry for this nice priest who had this outpost to defend with such meagre ammunition—nothing but a kindly smile in face of the most miserable poverty. But he didn't seem to bother much about the Indians' hostility to him.

Unfortunately for our researches, all the church records and documents had been burnt a few years previously, when the population of Jesus de Machaca had risen against the priest of the day. Such risings had not been infrequent here. Three times between 1930 and 1940 there had been revolts against the Church. The first time, the priest was executed and the Indians, having eaten the body, drank their native brandy out of his skull. The second time, the priest just managed to save his life by holding up the crucifix of the church, which seems to have daunted his assailants.

Such stories as these brought home to us the difficulty of our task, which was to break down the barriers of reserve and suspicion and probe the secrets of the Indian mind.

We called on the *corregidor* early in the morning, hoping to get something out of him before he was completely pickled. He did manage to enumerate the various communities under his charge, but that was all we could extract from him.

Our first attempts at conversation with the Indians were painful. It seemed as though nothing but a miracle would make them open up, but we were determined to push on with our inquiries.

What was a community? Was its structure religious or political, or simply a matter of kinship? How did these institutions work and how did they compare with modern communal organizations such as, for instance, the *kolkhoz* or the *kibbutz*?

When Sunday came, we saw several Indians by the church wearing almost luxurious *ponchos*, the classic *lluchos*, and holding black batons that were encircled by rings of silver and gold. They came and went in twos and threes, plying between the church and the *corregidor's* house, or sitting for hours at a time chewing coca leaves. Now and again, from an inside pocket, one of them would produce a bottle of spirits and hand it round. At twelve they went in for the mass, or rather about fifteen of them did, and apart from a couple of children they constituted the whole of the congregation.

The lieutenant went up to one of the remaining ones.

"*Ilacata*," he said, "I'm holding you responsible for the theft of a sheep from one of the neighbouring communities. It was one of your community which took it. I'm fining you 2,400 bolivianos and giving you a week to pay."

The *Ilacata* did his best to argue his way out of it. A strange creature. As he spoke, he held his baton in his hand.

We decided to question him with Aramayo's help.

"*Ilacata*, what community do you come from?"

"Cuypa."

"How old are you?"

A consultation ensued with the other *Ilacatas*, after which he told us he was thirty. That, we knew, was only an approximation. Among these Indians no one knows his age exactly; no one's birth is recorded; and no one could read the record if it were.

"How long have you been an *ilacata*?"

"From the first of January this year."

"And how long will you be one?"

"Till the first of January next year."

"How do people recognize your authority?"

He held up his baton, which was something over eighteen inches long. It was of black wood and mounted with six silver rings placed at regular intervals. Some other *ilacatas* showed theirs too, all about the same length, all provided with chased silver rings. These were the emblems of their power, without which they were in no way distinguishable from their neighbours, but bearing which they became at once the religious and political chiefs of their communities, wielding an authority that was both indisputable and undisputed.

It was arranged that we should visit the *ilacata* in his community the next day. He obviously didn't want to be drawn out any further in front of the others.

.   .   .   .   .

First thing next morning, he called for us, to take us to Cuypa. We had decided to take him in the jeep, and he was delighted.

"What's your name?"

"Warachi."

Warachi means 'the stars weep'. It is the name of a very old Indian family whose ancestors belonged to an ancient aristocracy.

This morning he wore a white *poncho* of hand-woven wool. This loose garment makes movements easy and keeps out the bitter cold. It has even been adopted by white men for use on horseback as it enables the reins to be held without the hands being exposed. Warachi's *llucho* was red, with a green woven pattern round it and a green llama in front. His attire was completed by white woollen trousers, also hand woven. He wore no shoes. His bare feet were hardened by the stony tracks. At his heels, cracked by the cold, you could see the thickness of the horny layer. Though they were obviously used to it, we couldn't imagine how his feet could stand the cold, and we gazed at him in astonishment.

As for his insignia, besides the baton, he had a silver cross on his breast, hanging from a string of coloured beads, and, coiled on his shoulder, a whip of plaited bull's pizzle.

Warachi was much like the other Indians we had met, of medium height, with prominent cheekbones, and a slightly copper-coloured skin. Only one thing surprised us, a faint downy moustache, a thing quite unusual among his race, in which hairiness is normally confined to an abundant head of black hair.

    •   •   •   •   •

This was the first time we had got down to serious ethnological research, and we were reminded of an oft-repeated saying of our teacher, Griaule: 'Nothing is so like a policeman as an ethnologist; the only difference being that the person interrogated is not a suspect, or at any rate not until he starts telling lies.'

As we drove along, we ran through the questions that seemed to us important. We decided we must check such information as we had already received.

"We must ask for the names of the various communities. It's no good asking how many there are, as we'll get a different answer every time."

"Exactly. Then, if they forget one, we can call their attention to it."

"How many do we know for certain?"

"For certain? We don't know anything for certain. I've got twenty-two names down so far. But Flores says Pueblo is also a 'community'."

Flores was the cantor.

We weren't surprised by this vagueness, for we had been up against it from the first, and it didn't seem to make much difference whether our informants were whites, Indians, or half-castes. As for the number of communities in the district, we had first of all been told six, then ten, then fifteen.

And there was some difference of opinion as to whether certain communities, part of whose names were identical with others, were true communities or merely sub-divisions.

We continued our discussion after alighting from the jeep, when, led by Warachi, we climbed up to Cuypa, scaling the stone walls that separated one field from another exactly like it. Warachi climbed quickly. Now that he was on his own territory, his manner towards us changed. He was full of attention. He was our host.

He took us to a little square in front of a church, where he left us for a few minutes. We sat down on a low stone wall, which surrounded a tree.

We were now in the heart of a community, excited to think that our real work was starting.

The squat mud-built houses straggled down the hillside towards the Jesus de Machaca road, their clumsy thatched roofs making them seem even lower than they were. Long walls of loosely piled stones cut across the arid waste of the Altiplano.

The walled square, empty at this time of the day, had a cob-built *reposoir* at each corner. Through archways in the mud walls we could see other houses and pens walled with unbaked bricks for sheep or llamas.

Everything was the same earthen colour, a slightly reddish brown, in fact, except for the loose stone walls, which were practically black, that was the colour of the whole landscape.

The jeep waited in the road below, the Macho standing by, but too far off for us to see what he was doing.

We were plunged deep in our thoughts when Warachi came back with two other men, each of whom carried a baton, though less richly ornamented than his.

Warachi explained that one of them was an *ilacata*, while the other was an *alcade*, elected for one year, whose job was to act as a liaison officer between the *ilacatas* and the official hierarchy above.

"Can anybody be an *ilacata*?"

"No. Only the wisest and most respected. They are elected a year or two in advance. In reality everyone in the community becomes an *ilacata*."

"You're elected for a year—what happens if one of you dies during his period of office?"

"His eldest son takes over and finishes the year, or sometimes his wife does."

We got down at last to drawing up a list of the communities. Spurred by our questions, Warachi gave us all the names quite accurately and easily.

It turned out that Pueblo, where the church and the authorities were to be found, was indeed a community, bringing the number up to twenty-five. It came as a surprise to us that the number should be an uneven one, as we had learnt in our university training that the communities were generally divided into two equal groups. Pueblo, which means village, was the only one to have a Spanish name. It is probable that when the conquerors founded the Church they created at the same time a new community.

There was no sign of the bi-partite structure we had been looking for. The Indians seemed to know nothing about it. It exists all right, but we were only to find that out later.

We soon realized it was useless to ask Warachi questions of a general nature. Having drawn up, at least provisionally, a list of the communities, we decided to ask him about the functions of an *ilacata*, who enjoyed, or so we had read, absolute power during his year of office.

"Warachi, who elects *ilacatas*?"

"The *ilacatas* of the previous year."

"All of them?" I asked.

"Yes."

"Have they each an equal voice?"

"Yes."

"And what are your powers?"

"I'm the *ilacata*."

"Yes, but what does that mean in practice?"

Warachi seemed not to understand. Obviously we weren't framing our questions in the right way.

I tried again.

"What do you do when you're an *ilacata*?"

"I go to see the *corregidor*."

"What about?"

"About the barley."

After a few more volleys of questions, Aramayo explained that the Indians had to supply fodder for the Bolivian cavalry.

"It's a levy," he said, "and all have to contribute. After negotiating with the *corregidor*, the *ilacata* has to apportion the levy amongst the members of his community. Although they're paid for the barley, it's none the less an imposition, and the Indians hate it."

"Do you also have to pay money-taxes, Warachi?" asked Jean-Luc. "Never."

This dialogue gives an idea of the progress an ethnologist makes when dealing with a mentality of a different order from his own.

At this point Warachi volunteered the information that no one could become an *ilacata* unless he had first been an *alcade*, which is also called *escribano* (writer) though none of the Indians can read or write.

We had read that an *ilacata* had no power unless carrying his insignia and Warachi confirmed this, but we were soon to learn something we had not heard before.

I asked Warachi to show us his house, and he took us past the church and up to a sort of yard, enclosed by loose stone walls, at the end of which were three tawny cob-walled huts which seemed to form a single group. One was the bedroom, one the kitchen, and the third another room. As a matter of fact, people seemed to sleep more or less everywhere, and the cooking was done as often as not in the open. As we approached, we saw heaps of a sort of millet called *quinoa* which were drying in the sun. Further on, spread over a sort of platform of beaten earth, potatoes were awaiting the frosts which would turn them into *chuño*.

Warachi took us into his bedroom. The walls, as we have said, were of cob, a mixture of mud and dried grasses, such as was still being employed twenty years ago in Normandy and the Sologne, using the method called in France *en caisson*, for which the Indians use the Spanish word *topaliera*. They knead the wet cob with their feet. Often they use stone foundations. Sometimes, instead of cob they use adobe. There is thus no standard type of building. Each hut is rectangular. Unlike their French counterparts they have no wooden framework; timber is so scarce and has to be brought from so far that it is reserved for the rafters. The tree under which we had been questioning Warachi was a rarity.

Even in the roof, wood is used as sparingly as possible, and is often reinforced or replaced by V-shaped pieces of cob whose arms are about two inches in diameter and a yard in length. This device, which seems to be of recent importation, shows the resources to which men are driven by shortage of materials.

The thatch, uncovered on the inside, was about eight inches thick.

There was nothing in the room which could properly be called furniture. The bed was simply a raised platform of earth about one foot high, four and a half feet wide, and six feet long, that being the whole depth of the room. It was covered with skins, blankets, and clothing.

"What do they call a bed in Aymara?" we asked Aramayo.

"*Ikiña.* Sometimes *patajati*, which means literally 'sleeping-thing'."

We moved to the hut which served as kitchen. The stove was in a corner. The pots and pans were on the floor or on earthen ledges. Fuel, consisting of *tola* and llama dung, was stacked at the end of the room opposite the stove.

The oval stove was about sixteen inches wide, eight deep and one foot high. Two holes in the top were for the cooking utensils, and another in front for draught and stoking.

It was a poor room and a sad one, in which it would be decidedly difficult to provide dishes for the gourmet.

We went back into Warachi's bedroom and sat down on the bed.

At the side of the house we had noticed a platform of beaten earth about six feet square and three feet high, covered by a dome, the top of which was six feet from the ground. We asked what it was for.

"It's an oven," said Warachi, "for baking bread, but it's only used for a *fiesta*."

The bed we were sitting on was hard, and we could feel the compacted earth through the skins and blankets.

In the middle of the room was a three-foot cube of beaten earth which I examined while Jean-Luc was trying to get Warachi to agree to having his photograph taken with his *ilacata* insignia. This cube was not in any way remarkable, but it was covered with a woollen drugget folded in two and containing coca leaves. We knew already that the Indians called it a table. Moreover, its presence in every Aymara house deprived it of any exceptional character.

The problem was what purpose it served. To me it seemed utterly useless, as nothing was ever on it, objects being invariably put on the floor, clothes thrown on the bed or hung on the walls.

"What's this table for?" I asked.

A relation of Warachi answered:

"It's the *ilacata's* table."

"Yes, but what's it for?"

"It can't be moved."

Indian wearing a *Llucho*

Warachi, Ilacata of Cuypa, wearing his Insignia

Having failed to make myself understood, I started off on another tack.

"Why can't it be moved?"

"Because it's the *ilacata's* table."

"What would happen if it was moved?"

"It can't be. Not while he's the *ilacata*."

"Why not?"

"He'd lose his power."

Intrigued by these somewhat frustrating answers, I recalled what M. Griaule had said about the chiefs, and also his advice always to drop a line of inquiry that seemed to be leading nowhere, following any other opening that might offer itself.

"Supposing the table was damaged while Warachi was *ilacata*, could it be mended?"

"No."

"Could another be made to replace it?"

"No. It mustn't."

"If someone did anything to the table, what would happen?"

"No one would. The *ilacata's* table has to stay just as it is."

"All the same, supposing someone did?"

"They wouldn't."

We were up against a typical example of Indian mentality. They cannot discuss anything hypothetical. What is outside the realm of actual experience has no significance whatever.

At the same time we had glimpsed another sidelight on the position of the *ilacata* in his community. We understood that if the Indians are so attached to this institution, it is because it symbolizes their unity.

We had come to Jesus de Machaca at a time when agrarian reform was the order of the day. Of Bolivia's total population—three and a half million—more than three million are Indians. That means that no movement can succeed without their co-operation.

The Indian has become conscious of his power. He knows that nothing can rob him of his conquests. The arms which he obtained legally at the time of the dissolution of the army are a constant anxiety to the former masters. They realize that you cannot for ever hold down people who have received military training, and, foreseeing an uneasy future, many of them are leaving their *fincas* for La Paz, or even settling abroad.

In the areas around Lake Titicaca, for instance, where land tenure is not unlike the *métayage* of France, the Indians are moved at one

C

moment by genuine devotion to their masters, while at the next they are being turned against them by political agitators. That is a phenomenon which may be found, of course, wherever revolutionary situations prevail.

At Jesus de Machaca the Indians are well organized. The community system, which at one time seemed to be on the downgrade, is now, under the influence of agrarian reform, as vigorous as ever. Nothing could be more misleading than to regard the *ilacatas* as mere survivals. Their office has acquired a new meaning.

Warachi hailed the Macho, who now joined us.

"Tell them we're taking the Finca Corpa," he said. "The Land Reform is giving it back to us, because it was stolen from us when the Spaniards came."

We knew that the *ilacatas* of old had been chiefs endowed with far greater powers than they enjoy today. In bygone times they had parcelled out the fields which each tenant had tilled in turn for a period of one year. They had administered justice as well as being religious heads. But all or nearly all of that has gone.

Their powers have waned. Yet neither the centuries of persecution, the encroachments of central governments, nor the intervention of the priesthood, have been able to dislodge from the hearts of the people their respect and attachment to their own native *ilacatas* who symbolize their unity and who treat with the authorities of the state. For his brothers, the *ilacata* still exercises the religious and juridical authority represented by his insignia.

Still more important is his mythical role. For years Mme. Germaine Dieterlen has been teaching the importance of myths. We now found ourselves in the presence of a clear-cut phenomenon—the *ilacata* was the incarnation, the living symbol of social unity.

An *ilacata* should be a man who has shouldered all the responsibilities of life. He should be a complete adult in the sense that he should be married, and, in some regions, a father too.

The co-optation by existing *ilacatas* of their successors showed that on important occasions the whole body of twenty-five communities could act together. Each community, grouped round one of their own members, allows the latter to be chosen by a larger body. It was in the light of this fact that we were able to understand the Indians when they said: Jesus de Machaca—twenty-five communities, or San Andreas de Machaca—six communities.

The bond between the different communities, often so weak (a

horse or a llama that has strayed across a boundary may be sufficient
to arouse hostility), suddenly comes to the surface at these cardinal
moments of social life.

If one of them is guilty of a misdemeanour, the whole community
will rally around him. Police matters and the administration of justice
may have been wrenched out of their hands: they have never been
renounced. Even today, they hate to see the white man or the *cholo*
(half-caste) interfere in what they consider to be their affairs.

A scene we had witnessed a few days previously will serve as an
example. A policeman attended a funeral, on the look-out for a
delinquent. This policeman was an Indian who came from one of the
communities of Jesus de Machaca. No sooner did he open his mouth
than an uproar broke out.

"He's a rotter. He was born here, like us, but he's lazy, so he joined
the government to live without working. All he wants is to make
trouble for us. Go away, you dirty skunk, or one of these days we'll
cut 'them' off for you."

The policeman went, but it was some time before the excitement
died down. The Indians were quite beside themselves, so outraged that
they even called on us to witness the enormity of it, though heaven
knows the white man's prestige is low enough in their eyes.

.   .   .   .   .

We had been questioning Warachi for hours, and though he was as
sweet-tempered as ever, he was obviously tiring. We decided this was
enough for one day, but we meant to come back to see him again. We
returned hungry to Jesus de Machaca, where the priest welcomed us
with his friendly smile, and I set to at once to make a meal. Meanwhile
the priest complained of his inability to stop the Indians putting
death's-heads in the church.

"I even find them on the high altar and spend my time taking them
up to the gallery. At first I used to do the same with all the little plaster
animals, but I've given that up."

We saw them for ourselves—plaster figures of sheep, cows, and
donkeys, and almost every day death's-heads that came from no one
knew where.

The little animals are not hard to explain—*ex votos*, placed there
either in gratitude for a boon received or to implore a favour, such as
fecundity to the owners' flocks. There is nothing unusual about this.

The Spanish hang up as *ex votos* in their churches wax effigies of parts of the human body, arms, legs, heads, etc., and the Brazilians do the same with women's breasts. The skulls are more puzzling. The origin of the custom has yet to be discovered. The police lieutenant told us (and we confirmed it ourselves) that the Indians re-inter bones that come to light when they dig graves.

We were aware, moreover, of the existence of a certain number of *chulpas* within the boundaries of Jesus de Machaca, *chulpas* being tombs of Inca or even pre-Inca period.

Several times we tried to probe the Indians about these skulls, but it was a subject they did not care to talk about and they always evaded our questions.

We discussed it amongst ourselves at night as we tucked ourselves away in our sleeping-bags.

"Do you remember Huancane near Khonkho? That was a site dating from before the Incas. When we got there someone told us that the Indians had rifled a *chulpa*, leaving clear signs of their excavations. Mightn't the skulls have come from there?"

"If they don't come from the cemetery, it's the only explanation."

"I don't think they come from the cemetery. We've never seen Inca bones there, while those in the church are undoubtedly Inca."

"On the other hand, the Indians have great respect for the *chulpas*. They say that anyone desecrating one will be transfixed by the bones of the dead man, who will 'rob him of his soul'."

It was a good deal later that an old schoolmaster told us that the skulls came undoubtedly from the *chulpas*.

III

The Last of the Urus

A FEW days later we decided to make a trip to a distant community called Lower Ankoaki.

"You'll be seeing some Urus," said Aramayo.

We knew that the Urus were a very ancient people (the first perhaps to settle round Lake Titicaca) who were now dying out.

"Where is Ankoaki?" we asked the priest.

"Although it's part of my parish," he answered, "I haven't yet been able to go there. It's a long way off. Flores is the man to ask."

At six in the morning, when the cantor arrived, he told us:

"Lower Ankoaki is on the banks of the Rio Desaguadero. I haven't been there for ages. It's a very long way and not at all easy going."

Nobody was being very encouraging, but that didn't deter us. Flores told us how to get there, and we took our leave, warning the priest we shouldn't be back till nightfall.

"There's plenty of game on the Rio Desaguadero," said Aramayo. "We'd better take our guns."

"What sort of game?" I asked eagerly.

"Lots of ducks and flamingos."

The Macho filled up the radiator, which had been drained for fear of frost, and off we drove.

"The Desaguadero runs into Lake Titicaca, doesn't it?"

"Yes. It comes from the Poopo."

"I remember now," said Jean-Luc, "we saw it from the train. That's where there was so much mirage."

We first took the road to Guaqui, turning off to the left a little below the Finca Corpa where we had slept on the night of our arrival. What we were now on was no more than a track, and before long it disappeared altogether, lost among the tufts of dry grasses.

"I know it's straight in front of us," said the Macho. "Watch the mountains for me and keep me on my course. I have to keep my eyes on the ground ahead."

Even in four-wheel drive, the jeep made heavy weather of it. There were few people about in that immense wilderness. If we did see anyone we made straight for him.

Coming upon an Indian soldier, we asked:

"Where are you going?"

"To Ankoaki."

"Jump in."

I moved up to make room for him and on we went again. Soon the stranger began talking.

"I've got eight days' leave," he said, "but I've been four days getting here, and it'll take me as long to get back, so I shan't have much time at home."

"You've come on foot all the way?" asked Aramayo.

"Yes."

"What? Eight days walking to spend one night at home!" Jean-Luc exclaimed.

The Indians were all like that, Aramayo told us in French.

"They'll walk for days on end for a purpose that seems to us quite out of proportion to the trouble involved. To sell a bushel of salt, they'll load up their llama and go a hundred miles. By the time they're back all the money they've made has gone by the way. As a matter of fact, they don't always do it that way. Sometimes they pool the business, one man going off with a whole convoy of llamas laden with salt. But if you go to Potosi or any other mining district you'll find Indians going off on long journeys for the most curious reasons."

"Since you come from Ankoaki," said the Macho, "you can help us find the way. It's over there, isn't it?" he added, pointing ahead.

"I think so, but I'm not sure. On foot I know the way all right. In a car everything looks different."

Sometimes, amid the tufts, we saw a round patch of white, looking like snow. If you go duck-shooting in France you can find the same sort of thing on marshy land.

Aramayo explained that in the rainy season the Desaguadero overflowed its banks, covering the plain we were traversing, which was only slightly higher than the normal water level. The river water is full of sodium sulphate and other salts, and as it dries off these white deposits are left.

We had been driving several hours when at last the landscape ahead changed. We could see we were approaching a broad yellow plain, unrelieved by any vegetation. Further on was the blue line of the Desaguadero.

Reaching the new ground, the jeep shot ahead. From the river bank we could see thousands of ducks and other birds. In the shallows, the pink flamingos stood absolutely motionless, save now and again when one of them would lazily stretch a wing or turn its head to preen itself.

To the left, on higher ground, were the first houses of Ankoaki, cob-built, like those I have already described. As we reached them, the church tower came into view, then the whole building.

The situation of the village was a sufficient explanation of the presence of Urus, who are fishermen. We were particularly curious to see them, having learnt from Professor Vellard—who had studied them thoroughly—that few were left and all of them now very old. Formerly the level of Lake Titicaca was much higher than it is today, some thirty feet or more higher in all probability, its shore extending to Tiahuanaco. Its retreat from the Urus' villages ruined the latter, who had to find other means of subsistence or migrate elsewhere.

Contrary to their usual behaviour, some of the Indians came up to our car, reassured no doubt by the presence of one of their community among us. We made contact with them quite easily.

"We'd like two *balsas* to go duck-shooting in," said Aramayo in Aymara.

Two Indians went off to find people with boats prepared to take us on the river.

Most communities do not like strangers to visit their churches, which are really no more than chapels. When asked, they generally reply that the man who looks after it is away and has taken the key with him. At Ankoaki, however, they made no difficulty whatever, and the door was promptly opened.

The interior was wretched, the cob walls flaking away. A rickety altar was covered with paper table-cloths, and on a corner of it a human skull was awaiting the resurrection.

"But where are the Urus?" we asked.

"There's only one left now. Her brother died four months ago. He was a hundred and ten."

"And what age is she?"

"About the same."

They pointed her out to us—a very old woman, sitting on the ground in the sun. Though her hands were quite incredibly dirty, the wool she was spinning was immaculate. Her clothes were different from those of the Aymaras. Unlike the latter with their black skirts and voluminous shawls, she wore a dark brown dress, with such tight sleeves that they may well have been sewn up on her, a thing done by many Indians in the cold regions. She allowed us to approach but hardly spoke to us. The fact was she understood and spoke very little Aymara.

Jean-Luc wanted to photograph her, but as soon as she saw his camera she made off at full speed and hid in one of the houses. An Aymara went after her to try to persuade her, but she remained inflexible, maintaining that every time she'd been photographed she'd fallen ill.

She had never married, nor had her brother, Raphael. Professor Vellard knew them personally and we brought him news of Raphael's death; he told us that their celibacy hadn't stopped either of them from having children, who, incidentally, had died. Knowing that she had already come within the orbit of Professor Vellard's studies, we left her in peace.

The social structure of the community was the same as that of the others we had visited; only, the proximity of the river had made it inevitable that the people of Ankoaki should be fishermen and bird-catchers. The birds are stalked at night, with the aid of lights, and taken quite easily. They are free for all, as South America has not reached the stage at which game laws become necessary.

Their boats are the famous *balsas*, made of *totora*. As a matter of fact *balsa* is a misnomer, being properly the name of a tree, the wood of which, extremely light, is used for making rafts, such as we were to make use of later in the forests. *Totora* is a reed which grows abundantly round Lake Titicaca and along the river.

The *totora* is cut by the Indians and first soaked. Then it is dried in sheaves, which are afterwards made up into long fusiform bundles; finally, these bundles are lashed together to form a boat of somewhat gondola-like appearance.

Two Indians came up and spoke to Aramayo.

"They've found two *balsas* for us," he explained. "I'll take Jean-Luc with me. Bernard and the Macho will go in the other. Like that, we'll have an interpreter in each craft. While Bernard and I are shooting, Jean-Luc can be taking photos and films."

We went down to the river and got into our respective boats. The guns took station in the bows; the boatman, his trousers rolled up above the knees, stood aft, armed with a long pole for punting. The *balsa* is a somewhat disconcerting craft at first acquaintance. It heels over at the least touch, and with every thrust of the punt-pole seems about to capsize. One soon finds out, however, that it has far greater stability than most boats.

I had my eye on the flamingos. Aramayo, long since *blasé*, made straight for where the ducks were most thickly clustered. The Bolivians like to bag as many birds as possible with a single cartridge. They haven't the European taste for difficult shots.

My *balsa* glided forward silently. The flamingos were still far off and I was afraid of missing them and hitting a cow. There were many cows about, wallowing in the water up to their chests, browsing on the river grasses, thrusting their muzzles into tufts that looked like huge green sponges.

The flamingos were getting nearer. Aramayo fired.

"I've got six," he said to Jean-Luc, his words coming clearly across the still water. "That's not many. Sometimes I get as many as twenty."

"Seems pretty good to me," came the answer. "You must be a mighty fine shot."

I groaned inwardly, afraid the shot would drive off the flamingos, which were just coming within range.

"Macho," I whispered, "don't you think I'm close enough?"

"Not quite. Take aim and I'll tell you when to fire."

I could now make out the red wings of the male birds. Squatting cross-legged in the bow, I aimed at one in the middle of the group, to allow for the spread of the shot.

"Are you ready?"

"Yes."

"Shoot."

The shot rang out. The flamingo in the middle fell, then another. The remainder didn't wait for a second shot. Flying in a flock, they were a wonderful sight in the sky. I fired again as they flew over the *balsa*, but they were too high and this time I missed.

The two wounded flamingos were struggling in the water. I told Macho to ask the boatman to go to them, but the latter refused.

"Better go for the ducks."

It's no easy matter to make an Indian change his mind. The Macho reassured me.

"Your flamingos won't get away. Try and get a few ducks before Aramayo drives them all off."

I followed his advice. The *balsa* approached the ducks. I fired.

The two *balsas* were now so close together that conversation between them was easy.

"I've quite fallen for this *balsa*," I said.

"They don't make a sound. Marvellous for duck-shooting. I'd like to take one back to France."

"Yes, they're wonderful. But how on earth would you carry it? We've baggage enough as it is."

All the same, we asked how much one cost. Four thousand bolivianos—barely three pounds! There's a regular trade in these craft. Made at Lower Ankoaki, they are taken down the river to Lake Titicaca, where they are sold, the vendors returning to their village on foot.

We had learnt in the other communities that the *ilacata* doesn't work, his work being done by members of his family. Here, however, by the side of a lagoon, we saw a man preparing *totora*.

"He's the *ilacata*," said the Indian with us.

"Of Ankoaki?" I asked.

"Yes," answered the Macho, who was acting as interpreter.

A detail of some importance. Nothing is more interesting in ethnology than the exceptions, which may indicate ritualistic survivals or, on the other hand, new evolutionary steps. In this case it was the latter. Primordially the whole community worked for the *ilacata*; soon perhaps all the *ilacatas* will work too.

We drove home that evening with a heap of birds three feet high in the back of the jeep, some of which were to vary the diet of our friend the priest. We stopped at the Finca Corpa to have the flamingos plucked, hoping also to find the master of the house whom we had missed on our previous visit. He was still away, however, and it wasn't till long after that we met him finally at La Paz.

When we got back, the priest greeted us with:

"I've nothing for you to eat."

"Don't worry about that," I answered. "Just leave it to me."

And I set to and produced a repast that astonished the poor priest.

"Something very strange happened today," he told us. "Soon after you'd gone an Indian called. He'd walked nearly forty miles to see me. It was to ask me to say three masses for him on three successive days! I naturally asked him if he had no priest in his own village. He said yes, but he was too expensive."

The priest explained that there was a tariff fixed by the bishop—one hundred bolivianos for a mass—but that many of the native priests failed to observe it.

"Things get around very quickly in this country," he went on, "and when this Indian heard that I abided by the tariff, he decided to bring his custom here.

" 'But you have to buy food on the way,' I objected.

" 'Yes, Padre,' he answered, 'but in my village a mass costs two hundred bolivianos, so it comes cheaper all the same.' "

.　　　.　　　.　　　.　　　.

The next day, having decided to turn our attention to magic, we sallied forth in search of a sorcerer, asking any Indian we happened to meet. They merely laughed. When we insisted, they pretended not to know of any. We didn't believe them as we had been told by half-castes, *cholos*, that every community had some. The priest was not the one to help us. Naturally he was no friend of the sorcerers. He had talked to us readily enough on Indian customs in general, but had always shut up if we tried to lead him on to the subject of magic. Several times we had tried to explain to him why we were bound to be interested in the subject, but he had always relapsed into a slightly sulky silence. Actually, we had had a sorcerer at our elbows the whole time, in the person of the priest's manservant, but our friend only told us this at the moment of our departure. He told us then that he had found the man practising his rites in the kitchen.

Having no success with our inquiries, we had recourse to a stratagem. It was Aramayo's idea. He suggested that we should use Jean-Luc as a guinea-pig. Jean-Luc had been suffering from one or two minor troubles caused by the altitude and needed professional advice. The soldier who had come with us to Warachi's offered to help us once again.

"I've heard by chance that there are plenty of them at Yahouri San Juan," I said.

"Yes," said the soldier, "we might well try there."

We didn't feel we could turn to Warachi. He, too, had laughed at our questions, and we suspected him of being a sorcerer himself.

To reach Yahouri San Juan we took a short cut across the plain. We went on foot, and it was very hard going. It was difficult not to trip over the tufts of grass, and we had often to make wide detours to ford the muddy streams. As usual we saw practically nobody. That didn't mean there was no one about, for the Indians have a marvellous faculty of fading away when they spy strangers. If you kill a vicuna (whose skin is much coveted) the Altiplano will come to life in a moment, and if you try to pinch a sheep or a llama from one of the seemingly unattended herds, you'll find yourself surrounded by a hostile crowd in no time.

We passed farms and groups of huts, all shut or empty, but at last came upon an old couple; the man was pottering about round his house with a small child trotting after him, while the woman was spinning, at the same time keeping an eye on a herd of lambs. This Darby and Joan were most amiable. We talked about their animals, their age, their children (all dead), and then led up to the important question:

"Can you tell us where we can find a sorcerer?"

The man smiled, but said nothing.

"Our friend here is ill and wants to be cured."

That did the trick. We were told where one lived and went off to find him. After a while, during which we saw a runaway horse that no one could catch and a llama that had been injured the night before as an act of vengeance, our search was rewarded.

He was quite ordinary to look at, our wonder-worker, a short, thick-set Indian of about fifty. He received us quite cordially and Aramayo explained in Aymara what we had come for.

He took us into his hut. We sat down on the bed behind the table, on which was a blanket folded in two and containing coca leaves. In our honour, however, he wanted to use fresh leaves that had never been used before. He left us, returning a few minutes later with a large handful which he laid on a small woollen mat. Asking Jean-Luc for a coin from his pocket, he dropped it in the middle, then gathered up the four corners of the mat and knotted them, forming a sort of bag, which he made Jean-Luc place on his chest just over his heart.

He then began intoning long prayers, asking God to grant him the power of divination. He prayed, squatting cross-legged on the floor, his hands held up in supplication. Sometimes he bowed forward from the waist. The prayers finished, he took the bundle from Jean-Luc, opened it and found the coin, which he placed to one side on a corner of the mat.

Gathering up the leaves, he proceeded to scatter them, letting them flutter down one by one on the coin and all round it, noticing carefully both the shapes of the leaves and the pattern they made. A cluster of leaves, we learnt, means grief and tears.

Finally he said:

"Your illness is nothing. You'll soon get over it. But there's trouble in store for you, bad trouble. I can see you kneeling before a statue of the Virgin, praying and weeping. It may not be at once, but it'll come surely. Perhaps the car will break down. Or you may lose money. Troubles, anyhow."

"Is there any way of avoiding the troubles?"

"There is, but it's too late now. The priest has no more masses free. You might pay in advance for a thanksgiving mass later. That might work, that might ward off the troubles."

He said the same things over and over again. From the time he began divining, he seemed to be in a sort of trance.

No sooner had we left the sorcerer's hut than the soldier began talking.

"They know a lot of things, these sorcerers. They know what's coming in the future, and they can heal people much better than the doctors. A few weeks ago a friend of mine, a soldier like me, was wounded in a scrap with some Indians. He came back to his village in a high fever, with a broken arm and weak from bleeding. When he passed the sorcerer's house he was called in, and when the sorcerer had done his divining he said what he needed was lizards. What's more, the coca leaves had said just where he could find some, and he went off and found the lizards at once. Taking them home he sacrificed them, keeping only the heads, which he put in a mortar with sulphur and sugar and pounded into a paste. And he put the paste on my friend's arm, and it was quite well in a week."

"We've heard of their using lizard skins from the lieutenant."

"Yes," said the soldier, "they use lizards a lot. Particularly for coughs. They rip them up longwise and put them all round the person's chest, strapping them on with a cloth."

The soldier was a firm believer in this branch of medicine. He added:

"A man fell from his mule and got some of his scalp torn off. He went to the doctor. No good. The place began to fester. Then he went to the *kututo* . . ."

Aramayo interrupted to explain that *kututo* really meant male rabbit but was often used for sorcerers.

"The *kututo*," went on the soldier, "first drank a lot of strong drink. Then he jabbed his knife into the bad place to let out the pus. The *kututo* drank some more and then sucked the wound. He sucked three times, spitting afterwards. Then he had another drink and said to the chap: 'There you are—you're all right now, and I'm none the worse.'"

The soldier gave us other examples. If your hair's in bad condition, the sorcerers tell you to rub your head with stale urine. For serious stomach troubles they kill a dog, rip it open longwise, and apply it, still warm, to the patient's abdomen.

We decided to return to Cuypa to have another go at Warachi. The soldier said he was quite ready to come with us again.

Warachi greeted us warmly. We resumed our seats under the tree in front of the church. Seeing smoke rising from his house, we asked what was going on.

"We've been burning a dead man's clothes."

"Really? Why?"

Warachi repeated his lesson.

"A week after a person's dead, we burn his clothes. At that moment the soul of one of the people gathered round falls in the fire. Everyone sees it fall. And that person will die within the year. All the same we try to stop it."

"How?"

"By beating him a week later. With boots."

"Does it work?"

"Sometimes. Often he dies all the same."

Warachi then told us that in the community of Upper Ankoaki, if there are purple marks on a dead body, they think the person's been bewitched. In that case they don't have a funeral at once, as is the custom. They leave the body on the bed for twenty-four hours with a dim light burning. In the kitchen they lay food out so that the dead person can make a meal, and the funeral isn't held till the third day.

When we had exhausted this funereal topic, Warachi invited us to eat with him. In the afternoon we went on with our questions and were taken to visit several houses; we counted the llamas and sheep owned by each.

It was when leaving Warachi's house that I said to Jean-Luc:

"I don't mind betting he's one of them. He's got the same blanket with coca leaves in it. Just like the chap that treated you."

But Warachi never let on.

Finding him so well disposed towards us, we decided to question him about the next world.

Like all his race Warachi was a Catholic, that is to say, a nominal Catholic, but we had already found out at Jesus de Machaca that Catholicism in this part of the world was a thin veneer that peeled off in many places showing material of another fibre beneath. That afternoon we meant to prise up the veneer a bit further.

"Warachi, where do dead people go to?"

"They're there," he answered with a sweep of his arm which indicated that they were all round us.

He began talking. We had no need now to ply him with questions. He seemed to understand what we were after. And he told us how the dead went off on long voyages, and, on those occasions, could appear to us. They came and went silently, never speaking, but they could be recognized all right.

Rites surrounding birth were of special interest to us. So were beliefs on the subject of menstruation, whose importance had so often been emphasised by our masters, M. Griaule and Mme. Dieterlen. Warachi was just the man: he had obviously come to the conclusion that there was no harm in us and was perhaps a little flattered at being chosen as our informant.

It was on the subject of menstruation that we had our first little difficulties with our interpreter. When we asked what the women did about it, Aramayo answered at once without passing our question on. As a matter of fact, what he told us was perfectly true, but we wanted our information to come as far as possible from the Indians themselves. It took us quite a little time to explain this to him, the trouble being that we had touched on a subject that offended his delicacy. In the end, however, we persuaded him reluctantly to ask. The Indian women do nothing about it at all. They simply allow the blood to run down their legs, which they wipe with their skirts. They are subject to no prohibitions at this period and work exactly as at other times. Here at Cuypa menstrual blood was not used to make magic philtres, as we were to find with Indians elsewhere.

Childbirth, according to Warachi, was treated as a very simple matter. When she felt the first pains, the woman went home and some matron was sent for to help her. If the latter came too late, the husband would assist. For the matron would not be a real professional midwife and might well be away working in the fields. Midwifery was just a sideline, as it still is sometimes in the country in France.

When the child was born, the mother wrapped it up in some rags, and took very little notice of it. She would wash it a week later for the baptism, and that wash had to last a lifetime!

"What do they do with the afterbirth?"

Another indelicate question! Neither Aramayo nor the Macho wanted to pass it on. They assured us nothing was done with it, and hoped we would leave it at that. We were obstinate, however, and finally obtained this surprising answer.

"After the mother is delivered, the afterbirth is carefully washed till it is free from any trace of blood. It is then smeared with a gruel made of maize and *quinoa*, after which the husband hangs it up outside, under the eaves. When it is dry, it is either buried or burnt. If the latter, the ashes are buried in a field.

The object of this rite is obviously the fertilization of the soil, a close connection being made between human birth and the germination of seed.

We asked what was done when a woman died pregnant.

"She's buried," said Warachi, "and, after three days, dug up again. The *compadre* (a sort of godfather) has then to cut open the body, sewing it up again after the foetus is removed. The body is then buried again. So is the foetus, but a separate grave is dug for it."

"Does a woman take any precautions after confinement?"

"None whatever. She bundles up the child and goes straight back to work."

For many primitive people, the birth of twins is surrounded by numerous beliefs. At the time of our visit there were no twins at Jesus de Machaca, nor had there been for a very long time. If twins were born, it would be regarded as an event of great good fortune to the family concerned.

"How does a young man pay court to a girl?"

Warachi smiled—the Indians do not smile easily—and answered:

"He throws pebbles at her—small ones. If she likes him, she'll throw pebbles back. Then he comes closer. When he's quite near he pinches her, and she pinches him."

"Do engaged couples live together before being married in church?"

"Yes. Generally."

"Do they often have children before they're married?"

"Yes. Quite often."

The priest confirmed that later, telling us that he often married couples who came to the church with two or three children in tow, sometimes even more.

"Who asks for the hand of the girl?"

"The young man's father. He goes to the girl's father with a bottle of spirits, coca leaves, and cigarettes."

"Is adultery common?"

Warachi said it was. Apparently no one bothered much about it.

The sun was going down. Aramayo gave the signal for our departure, and we took leave of Warachi promising to see him again, either at Cuypa or at Jesus de Machaca.

Warachi's house

Warachi with members of his Community

IV

The Funeral

ON the day following our visit to the last Uru, we were getting ready to go off on a trip when the priest, coming back from the church, told us he had to conduct a funeral service that day. We promptly changed our plans, and, jumping into the jeep, drove off to meet the funeral *cortège*, which was coming from a place ten miles away. The death had occurred the previous day.

Flores, the cantor, had already told us what happened when a person died.

As soon as death is certain, everyone gathers round the deathbed and the wake begins. The number of people there depends on the quantity of alcohol available, or, in other words, on the wealth of the bereaved family. All night long they stay by the dead, drinking uninterruptedly. First thing in the morning someone goes off to tell the priest. Others roll the body in a *bayeta* (blanket) which is lashed up like a hammock. The gruesome bundle is then secured to a simple stretcher, made of two poles with a length of cord laced backwards and forwards between them.

The family and all the mourners then run with the body to the church. The family are dressed in mourning *ponchos*, which have three-quarter-inch yellow bands along the two sides, three-quarters of an inch from the edges.

We had only received vague instructions where to go, and started off in the direction of San Andres de Machaca. Seeing no sign of the *cortège*, we were on the point of turning back when we heard cries in the distance. Soon a group of people came into sight in the centre of which we could see a splash of orange. They were moving fast, raising a cloud of dust in the middle of the vast stretch of the Altiplano.

The Macho, who knew the region well, said at once:

"That's them. You can see the body covered with an orange blanket."

"But they don't seem to be coming this way."

"They're stopping."

Indeed the whole group had come to a standstill. The body was

49

clearly visible now. We saw them put it down; then the whole group sat round in a wide circle.

"What are they doing?"

"They're going to have a drink."

They sat there for twenty minutes, then got up abruptly, continuing their journey at a trot. By this time some stragglers had caught up, mostly women or old people for whom the pace had been too hot.

There was no doubt now where they were making for. They had taken a diagonal path, which joined the track leading to Nucleo Escolar. Turning the jeep as quickly as we could, we cut across to get ahead of them, and reached them just as they were turning into the track.

We were uncertain of our reception. Would they object to our presence on such an occasion? Even if they didn't, would they allow us to film it?

In a field, a few yards from the track, two women, who had been working there, squatted down and began praying for the dead, raising and lowering their hands as they did so. That is the Indian custom: anyone who sees a funeral *cortège* promptly stops what he is doing and offers up prayers for the rest of the dead man's soul.

Our welcome was not long in doubt. At the head of the *cortège* was a man we had already met. As soon as he saw who we were he called out to us joyfully. All the others followed suit; they came up to us, showing their pleasure by jumping into the air and whooping.

Now that we were close, Jean-Luc started filming. That delighted them still more and they clamoured to be given photos at once. The dead body was jolted up and down by the bearers. The lashing worked loose. Two feet appeared, the soles covered by a stiff piece of sheepskin fixed in position by strands of wool which passed between the toes. The form of the body was clearly visible through the orange blanket.

The excitement caused by our appearance soon wore off. The group moved forward again, hurrying as before. Occasionally there was a cry of "*Cambio, cambio*," in Spanish. It was the signal for a change of bearers, and the stretcher passed from shoulder to shoulder without any slackening of the pace. Jokes were bandied about and there was a lot of laughter.

"My word! The old boy's heavy. Take my place, will you?"

"How old was he?" we asked.

"At least a hundred and ten."

But an old man who spoke a little Spanish edged up to us and said in fits of laughter:

"He was very old. He was ten."

We had joined in the race, but without much hope of winning this Bolivian Marathon. We should have liked to be able to sweat, but the dry air prevented the skin giving passage to the least moisture. Soon we threw ourselves down by the side of the track panting for breath, our hearts pounding wildly, our heads throbbing, our whole bodies tingling most unpleasantly.

We sat there for quite a time getting our breath back, sometimes inexplicably losing it again. Little by little, however, our blood became reoxygenated. We had forgotten we were over twelve thousand feet up.

Quite untroubled by the altitude, the funeral party were more than half a mile ahead, but we could still hear their cries distinctly.

"*Cambio, cambio.*"

We got back into the jeep which bumped over the uneven track. The Indians sat down once again to have a drink. This time the dead man seemed quite forgotten, dumped down a few yards to one side of the circle. An old woman hurried across a field as fast as her short legs could carry her. She ran leaning forward, her big black and yellow shawl flying in the wind. Joining the others, she sat down and was given a drink.

Approaching Jesus de Machaca, we drove ahead to get to the church first. The priest was waiting in front of the door. It was there, he told us, that he would perform the ceremony. He didn't like to have the Indians inside, as they behaved so badly. A little while back, they had dropped a corpse completely naked in the aisle.

The cries approached. Then the *cortège* came into sight between the houses. We had just time to ask:

"Where had we better stand, Padre?"

"Anywhere. It doesn't make any difference. You'll see for yourselves they have no sense of decorum, no respect for the service. I have to call them to order all the time."

A little way off a handful of Indians stood waiting apathetically.

As they entered the square in front of the church, the bearers slackened their pace. Coming slowly up to the door, they put down the body wrapped in the orange *bayeta*. The priest told the congregation to be quiet, but it wasn't much good. They stopped talking for a moment, then broke out louder than ever. The priest's servant spoke to them one by one and made them sit down in a semicircle.

The cantor, who had drunk too much, began in a shrill voice to intone a psalm. He played the harmonium too—with plenty of false notes. The priest, quite at a loss, fumbled with his missal. Flores went on for ages, and the priest began to look anxiously at him, wondering whether he would ever have done. Finally, to put a stop to the psalm, which didn't belong to the service at all, he chanted:

"*Dominus vobiscum.*"

Flores went blandly on. The priest looked helplessly at us, though he couldn't help smiling.

At last the music stopped, but it didn't give place to silence. The Indians were getting impatient; they fidgeted and talked. To calm them down, the priest put them to saying their *Pater Noster* in Aymara. It didn't help much. They hardly bothered to repeat the words after him.

A woman got up, moved a little distance, then stooped without the slightest embarrassment to relieve nature.

"*Dominus vobiscum.*"

"*Amen,*" came the response from the cantor, but it wasn't the right one.

And during the final prayers, murmured softly, he forgot all about the responses and started singing. The Indians thought they'd had about enough. They stood up, unrolled the *bayeta* and lifted the body by its four corners. They were now all ready to go. The priest whispered to us:

"They're not as drunk as usual today. I'll go to the cemetery too."

He led the *cortège*, turning round from time to time to tell his followers to keep quiet. Now that the body was uncovered, we could examine it: an old man who seemed taller than most Indians; white hair, which had receded to leave a high forehead; white trousers; a white waistcoat laced up in front.

And the Indians went on laughing, shouting, joking, despite all the efforts of the priest. As soon as we arrived at the entrance to the cemetery, he gave his last benediction and hurried off.

The dead man was put down by the entrance. The mourners squatted in a circle again and had some more to drink.

The time passed. We wondered whether they were ever going to think of going inside. Aramayo spoke to them, then told us:

"They've sent someone for the key."

The man didn't come back. Presently Aramayo spoke to them again, and they sent another man after the first.

The time passed. Neither returned. Wandering round the cemetery, Aramayo and I found a breach in the adobe wall. We went through, opened the door from inside and told the Indians they could come in.

"Oh no. We must have the key."

"But the door's open. . . ."

"We must wait for the caretaker who keeps the key."

"What do you want the key for when the door's open already?"

"We have to pay 150 bolivianos for the key."

"We can pay it."

"That won't do. If we go in without paying we'll be fined 1,500 bolivianos."

There was no use going on. If we'd found an answer to that, they'd only have thought of something else. Aramayo and I went back into the cemetery and shut the door.

The caretaker arrived at last, tried to unlock the door, but couldn't. Once again Aramayo had to open it from inside.

The body wasn't picked up at once. Ignoring it, the party streamed into the cemetery. It was very small for a population of twenty thousand, no bigger than would be found in France for a village of two hundred. Each community had its bit of ground, a few square yards in area.

"We want a bigger cemetery," the Indians told us. "We've been asking for one for years."

What they really wanted, of course, was to be allowed to bury their dead in the soil of their own community. We knew that was impossible. The government would never leave them free to practise their own funeral rites.

The cemetery, called in these parts a *panteón*, was a jungle of weeds. We had never seen grass growing so high on the Altiplano. The priest would have liked to put his horse to graze on it, but couldn't because of the Indians.

"It would be disrespectful to the dead," they objected.

A few tombs of sun-baked mud bore witness to a rich family. On one was a child's skull, startlingly white.

The Indians were looking for a place in their allotment in which to dig the grave. They hesitated. One poked about with a pick, another with the tip of a spade.

At last they made up their minds. A man set to with the pick, but he hadn't been at it for more than five minutes when he passed the tool to someone else so that he could have a drink. Another, with the spade, removed the earth as it was loosened. He too had soon to be relieved for refreshment. And so it went on in a cycle, pick-drink-shovel-drink, hour after hour.

A lot of bones were unearthed, including no less than twenty-five skulls, each of which was the subject of innumerable jokes.

Jean-Luc played the part of professor of anthropology, explaining to the Indians how to tell a man's skull from a woman's, or a youth's from an old man's. He only needed a white overall to look the part to perfection.

A young man came up to us, working the mandible of a very fine specimen. It was the skull of a young man who couldn't have been dead long. None of the teeth was missing.

"I'm sure it's my brother," said the boy, convulsed with laughter. "He died young."

Some picked up femurs and compared them to their own, delighted if they found a good match.

When a skull appeared, they would shout at the man with the pick:

"Look out! If you smash it, you'll get your own smashed too."

Sometimes they played ball with the skulls. The ribaldry never ceased.

We were astonished to see the Indians laugh like that. Till then we had been struck above all by their gravity.

It was a slow business. Not only did the men work sluggishly, but when one threw down the pick to have a drink it might be quite a long time before another volunteered to take his place.

In fact it got progressively slower and slower. The diggers were tired and thought the grave was deep enough. A member of the family came forward to judge, and said it wasn't. A grave must be deep enough for a man standing in it to be concealed from the waist downwards. It must also have reached virgin ground, that is to say ground with no bones in it. And bones were still coming to light at every moment.

At last the requirements seemed to be fulfilled. The man standing in it was only visible from the waist upwards. Unhappily the next of kin insisted on another trying, and he was an exceptionally tall man. So, after a lot of argument, the digging went on.

When all was ready, the Indians went to fetch the body. Before it was lowered into the grave, some alcohol was poured in.

A near relative was then wrapped in a muffler so that only his eyes were visible. The muffler was to act as a respirator, protecting him against the 'bad air'.

This man, who had had a lot of drink, tried to get down into the grave, but lost his balance and fell full-length on the corpse. He raised himself slightly, and someone handed him a knife. With it, he cut the dead man's throat 'to let out the bad air and allow him to breathe'. That done, he scrambled out of the grave as fast as he could. Beside the body they laid a little ladder made of straw about a foot long, 'so that he could climb up to heaven'.

The grave was filled up as fast as possible. No sluggishness now. The sooner the grave's filled up, the sooner the dead man gets to heaven.

We left with the Indians. The afternoon was getting on and we were very hungry. The macabre spectacle we had witnessed hadn't interfered with our appetites. By the time we had prepared a meal and eaten it the day was too far gone for us to think of any further field work, so we spent the rest of it classifying the material we had collected.

.   .   .   .   .

First thing next morning we started out for Guaqui, where we were to do some shopping. The *padrecito* came with us, delighted to have an opportunity of hobnobbing with the priests of his order who had charge of the church there.

We weren't intending to stay long in the town ourselves. We wanted to go back to Ankoaki to see if we couldn't after all persuade the old Uru woman to have her photograph taken. We told the priest we would make a day of it, calling back for him in the evening.

After about twenty miles, we were forced to confess ourselves lost. The white patches of salt were all alike. The only thing we could do, the Macho said, was to forge straight ahead and hope for the best—as straight, that is, as it was possible to go in that country where you had to wind your way through the great tufts of grass. We drove in silence, somewhat anxious.

After hours of search, we saw a group of some ten or a dozen dogs grouped round a black object in the middle of a patch of salt. As we approached, the black object turned out to be an old man squatting on the ground. His clothes were quite different from the Aymaras'— close-fitting breeches of thick brown hand-woven wool, an upper

garment of the same colour whose short narrow sleeves seemed to
have shrunk.

"It must be an Uru," said Aramayo, "but what can he be doing
here, miles from any village?"

We got out from the jeep. Aramayo went up to the man, who
began to speak at once.

"I've been waiting for you. God told me some white men were
coming and would need me. I've been praying for you."

"Where's Jesus de Machaca?" asked Aramayo.

The old man pointed. Our anxiety was at an end. But we had to
give up the idea of going to Ankoaki, or the priest would be worrying
about us.

We got Aramayo to ask him some questions.

"He gave away everything he had to his children, who then
abandoned him so that he now has to beg. He lives by praying for
others."

"Is he an Uru?"

"Half Uru, half Aymara. He speaks Aymara quite well."

The Macho was impatient to be off, afraid we might get lost a
second time. So after giving the old man some money we returned to
Guaqui; we were rather late, but the priest had been enjoying himself
too much to notice it.

At Jesus de Machaca we found that the lieutenant had had the
bright idea of getting dinner ready for us.

.   .   .   .   .

Early the following morning the Macho dragged us out of our
sleeping-bags, telling us that there were Indians in the square who said
there was a blue mountain near their community out of which a thick
liquid was oozing.

"Oil, perhaps," he added.

We went off in the jeep, taking with us the Indians who had
brought the news. They sat in silence, their hats on their knees, their
ponchos thrown over their heads. Before long the car was filled with a
strong smell, a mixture of coca, alcohol, smoke, and dirt, which soon
permeated everything. It reminded us of our train journey from Buenos
Aires to La Paz in a carriage full of Indians with parcels of many
colours and baskets hanging from the roof, to the smells of which were
added, at the stations, the peculiar one of burning *tola* wood. It came

from the wood fires on which the Indian women cooked their highly spiced meats.

Our passengers directed the Macho to a little hill, at the foot of which we alighted. When they insisted on our climbing the hill, we bitterly regretted having come, for we knew well by now how painful the least gradient was at that altitude.

The mountain, when we saw it, was indeed blue, being of slate rock, though the Indians said it was due to its having been burnt by fire.

Sure enough they showed us a little trickling stream of dirty blackish water, but the colour was easily explained by the presence of pigs in the vicinity.

We laughed over our attempt at prospecting, but the Macho was quite disappointed.

We were near enough to Cuypa to be tempted to visit Warachi again. After all, we were there not to strike oil, but to find out something of the social organization of the natives, and we had still much to learn. No one had yet told us anything about the bi-partite division of the communities.

When we found him, we sounded him on the subject.

"Yes," he answered, "Jesus de Machaca is divided into two parts, Khonkho and Sulcatiti, each containing the same number of communities."

We drew up a list of them. Two columns, twelve in each.

"But Pueblo is a community too, isn't it?"

"Yes, but it doesn't belong to either Khonkho or Sulcatiti."

"Are they divided territorially?"

"Yes. In line with the road to Nucleo Escolar."

"Warachi, is any land farmed communally?"

"*Aynoka*," was the answer.

"What's *aynoka*?"

Warachi seemed to find that question tiresome. When pressed, however, he told us with quite good grace.

"The *aynoka* is when we all join together to till the land of one member of the community."

"Does everyone take a hand in the ploughing?"

"Yes, and the sowing too."

"Who provides the seed?"

"Everyone. Everyone brings some."

"And the harvest?"

"Each has his bit to do."

"How long does it last, an *aynoka?*"

"A year."

"Is all the land of that member of the community done that way?"

"No, only part."

We tried to get him to tell us what proportion, but with no success, until one of us scratched on the ground the plan of a field and asked him to mark off how much of it would be *aynoka*. He took the stick and marked off about a fifth of the area.

"Does everybody have to give land to the *aynoka?*"

"Everybody in turn."

That meant that in an average community the turn would come round once in eighty years, never more than once in a lifetime.

Aynoka is a word confined to the plains. The same custom in the mountains goes by the name of *kato*. Thus what had in the first place prompted us to undertake this journey was still in existence as it had been since time immemorial.

.   .   .   .   .

We wanted to have another look at Warachi's house to check some detail or other of its construction. As we walked towards it, he told us he was the owner of all the vestments used at the *fiestas*. All the communities around hired them from him when they celebrated the day of their patron saint. This stock represented quite a considerable capital, for some of them were covered with silver plaques or decorated with silver coins.

"You must come to our *fiesta* at Cuypa, and take part in it," he said.

Unfortunately the date was too far ahead for us to be able to accept. We consoled ourselves, however, with the hope that we might witness the great feast of the Virgin at Copacabana.

Warachi's wife, who had already noticed us, was waiting for us on the threshold. Her children no longer fled or hid behind her skirts, for we were by this time friends of the family.

Our hostess was dressed as usual—short black skirt, white bodice, bowler hat. It was only for great occasions that the women wore their numerous many-coloured petticoats.

We were presently joined by an *alcade* wearing a *poncho* striped with red, yellow, and brown. He asked us to take his photograph. That was a very good sign: it meant that local mistrust was disappearing. What a pity it was we had shortly to be moving on. Other Indians arrived and Jean-Luc photographed them gathered round the *alcade*, who was beside himself with joy.

When we told Warachi we were going back to La Paz, he pressed us to stay, begging us once more to take part in the Cuypa *fiesta*. Alas, we had to be firm. Other work was waiting for us in Bolivia, to say nothing of Peru. We were already beginning to be afraid of not reaching Peru till after the rains had started.

"But if we can get back for it, Warachi, we promise not to miss your *fiesta*."

Once again we admired his *ilacata's* baton.

"Will you have to hand it to your successor?"

"No. It stays in the family."

"Who was the first to have it?"

"My grandfather."

We sent the Macho to fetch a bottle of *pisco* from the jeep, to have a parting drink with Warachi, after which we said good-bye to our most useful informant, with the wish that his great-grandson might one day follow him in office.

.   .   .   .   .

Returning to La Paz we stopped once again at Corpa to pick up the skins of the flamingos we had left there.

We drew up at the gate of the *finca*, and began to look for the Indian with whom we had left them. Search as we might, we could find no sign of him, however. In fact the whole place seemed to be deserted, the houses empty. In the end, though, after a good deal of searching and calling, an Indian did appear.

"Where's the caretaker?"

"Gone to Guaqui."

"I don't believe you," said Aramayo. "I'm sure he's hiding. Where has he put our flamingo skins?"

"I don't know; he has taken all the keys with him."

"That isn't true; the doors of the courtyard and the kitchen are wide open."

The Indian smiled at this but made no answer.

"Go on. Find those skins for us."

The argument went on for quite a time, at the end of which Aramayo's persistence won the day. An Indian, who must have been listening, came up carrying the skins.

"You see what they're like," said Aramayo to us. "They could have given us what we wanted in the first place, but hoped to tire us out. They love flamingo feathers, which they make use of at their *fiestas*. In the end, when they see it's no use, they give up."

We left the district dreaming already of coming back one day. Jesus de Machaca is one of the most interesting centres in the country. The culture of the natives is still largely Indian, little transformed by white influence.

It mustn't be thought that the race is degenerate. The Indians chew coca and drink a lot of spirits, to be sure, but those are not signs of degeneracy. Infant mortality is appallingly high, but in all probability no more than it was before the coming of the Spaniards, unless the standard of living under the Incas was much higher. Judged by their physical development one would certainly be inclined to think the Indians a robust race. If they were not, they would hardly have been able to maintain themselves at such an altitude and in such bitter cold.

Lastly, in spite of all the dirt, the unbalanced diet, and lack of hygiene, many Indians live to the age of a hundred and fifteen. That isn't the sign of a dying race.

V

The Island of the Sun

WE got to La Paz in the middle of the afternoon. We had been working very hard on communities, and been constantly on the go; as a result both Aramayo and we ourselves felt we needed a rest.

What better place could there be to rest in than Copacabana, on Lake Titicaca?

It was impossible to go in the jeep, which needed an overhaul. The only other means of getting there, apart from hitch-hiking in lorries, much favoured by the Indians and sometimes even by the whites, was by *gondola*. One was leaving the following morning, returning in a day or two. A *gondola* in South America is a small bus which runs a more or less regular service.

The one we took was far from young, but it was not the first—the service had been running for twenty years.

There are two steamers on Lake Titicaca plying between Guaqui and Puno on the Peruvian shore. They are the *Ollenta* and the *Inca*, both British built. The lake is quite as accessible on the Peruvian side. In fact a road runs right round it, passing through Copacabana, which lies at the bottom of a gulf in the peninsula opposite the Island of the Sun.

The lake is indeed the best means of communication between Bolivia and Peru, the journey being by rail from La Paz to Guaqui and then, after the steamer crossing, by rail again from Puno to Arequipa.

Going by road, we by-passed Guaqui, making for Tiquina, to take the ferry across the Estrecho, the narrow stretch of water between the eastern shore of the lake and the Copacabana peninsula.

A little before Tiquina the landscape changed. We left behind the arid stretches of the Altiplano and entered hilly country. The road climbed, went through a pass, and there was the lake before us. Jolting over the uneven road, the *gondola* wound its way down. The hillside had been cut into terraces in Inca days. Respected by the Spaniards, these were still intact.

It was a beautiful scene and the weather was lovely. In the distance we could see the Peruvian shore. On the water a small fleet of *balsas* were trout fishing. The trout here are excellent, sometimes exceeding fifty pounds.

After Jesus de Machaca, it was strange and pleasant to feel ourselves tourists.

Tiquina. We stopped near the lake, and the driver asked us to get out. The *gondola* was crossing, too, but had to do so empty. Waiting for the ferry, we wandered about among the houses bordering the lake. In the brilliant sunshine, the lake seemed more colourful than ever, scintillating with a whole scale of greens and blues.

We had some beer in a little shop, and what was our surprise to find pictures of MacArthur on the walls! What strange fate had brought them here?

There were two ferry boats, one for passengers, the other for vehicles. They were much alike—sailing barges with brightly painted hulls.

We arrived on the other side long before the *gondola*, but that didn't make any difference: in any case we were stopping here for lunch. It had all been arranged beforehand by the driver of the bus. At the hotel, a red-haired Catalan took us to admire the enormous trout which seemed to be basking in the sun a few yards from the shore.

We were only too happy wandering about with no particular objective. The real tourists who were with us seemed to belong to another world, particularly an American photographer laden with cameras. He had been five years in Peru taking photographs for some New York illustrated paper. He didn't know a word of Spanish, and we wondered what fairy-stories he put as captions to his pictures.

There were also three Chilean girls (somewhat elderly ones) who affected a disdain not only for Bolivia but for all South American countries.

After lunch we rattled off once again in the *gondola*. The road climbed. Here and there it was bordered by tall, elegant eucalyptus trees. Up and up we went, passing thirteen thousand feet and still climbing, till we felt we were right in the sky. All round us was blue. We were on a ridge of the peninsula with the lake below us on either hand. The driver stopped for us to admire the view.

Everything seemed larger than life. The snow-capped mountains were shimmering in the distance, but through that limpid air they seemed quite close. In the lake, the Island of the Sun and the Island of the Moon were tinted red by the sun. Well could we understand how this scene had fired the imagination of the Incas and led them to make this their great religious centre.

It may even be that their treasures are in the safe-keeping of Lake Titicaca. According to Aramayo, the Emperors, cheated by the Spaniards, threw their wealth and their works of art into the sacred waters.

When the Inca travelled, his litter was surrounded by guards carrying a golden chain. One man to each link! It is that chain, more than all else, that men's minds hark back to when tales of treasure are told.

The *gondola* drove on, and it wasn't long before the town came in sight. The road went down in a series of hairpin bends, crossing and recrossing the old Inca road which was absolutely straight. The road is still used by the Indians, who drive their flocks of llamas on it, urging them forward with cries of "*Haya! Haya!*"

The llama is not an obstinate beast. On the contrary, unless maltreated, it is quite docile. As a matter of fact, the Indians are not cruel to their animals.

Copacabana. A small town grouped round a big Franciscan church which has an important monastery beside it.

In front of the church, a huge square with a few trees, a bandstand.

"It's here they hold their *fiesta*," said Aramayo. "I hope we'll be able to see it."

The buildings round it housed various authorities, academic and political, police, customs, etc. At the hotel, we settled everything as quickly as possible and went off to hire a boat to take us on the morrow to the Island of the Sun.

We were well received by the Lieutenant of Police, who, when he saw our papers, promptly put at our disposal an outboard motor-boat and two soldiers.

"If you take my advice, you'll make an early start. The island's much farther off than it looks. If you want to do it comfortably, you'd better leave at four."

Back at the hotel, which was by the lake, we saw that a jeep had just arrived. It was fitted with a wireless aerial at least fifteen feet high.

We at once made advances to the occupants, an Argentinian and a Colombian. They were on their way to Colombia, having come from the Argentine, with whose political régime, we gathered, they had little sympathy. It didn't take us long to make friends with these two, whose names we learnt were José and Manuel. There is no need to mention their surnames.

We went to see the church, which we found less interesting than those we had seen in places off the beaten track. Originally in colonial style, it had been restored and added to, not always happily, the trouble being that the pilgrims coming here to pray to the Virgin leave quite a lot of money behind them, and it has willy-nilly to be spent. We had noted the same elsewhere: the shrines to which pilgrims trek are more redolent of faith and fervour than of beauty.

Behind the high altar was a chapel, between which and the nave was a window that served as a niche for the miraculous statue of the Virgin. An ingenious mechanism enabled her to be turned either towards the church or the chapel.

The curtain was drawn now and the figure faced towards the chapel. To reach the sanctuary we had to pass through a number of passages and staircases. It was full of Indians, pilgrims, and tourists. Our Chilean women were there, kneeling. The Virgin was really beautiful, carved by an Indian out of wood, which gave her a bronzed complexion. She was dressed, Spanish fashion, in white silk, and had a halo of silver and gold with a diadem encrusted with precious stones.

When we had finished admiring it we asked for an audience with the Father Superior of the Franciscans. It was readily accorded and he showed us a beautiful ivory crucifix.

"It's Spanish work and was brought here in colonial times."

"Does the Virgin perform many miracles?" one of us asked.

"A great many. She grants practically everything that's asked. If you have a wish to prefer, come back this evening after seven o'clock. You give fifty or a hundred bolivianos and the Virgin's cloak is placed on your head. It's then that you must wish. At a pinch you could go two together, but no more, as the cloak isn't big enough."

"Jean-Luc, now's the chance for you to have the sorcerer's prophecy fulfilled."

This somewhat irreverent remark of mine was made in a confidential whisper, however.

"Does the Virgin keep the same garments all the time?"

"No. They are changed once a year. For dust gets into the niche in spite of its being glazed on both sides."

"Could we witness it?"

"Oh no! Only monks are admitted to the ceremony."

We left with many pamphlets, both religious and historical. On examining them, we found them to contain more homilies than facts, and we were unable to learn much of the history of Copacabana.

We looked at the shops. I asked for a chemist's. There wasn't one,

Aramaya in a Balsa on Lake Titicaca

Balsas on Lake Titicaca

Old Aymara couple directing us to a Sorcerer

but a woman in a little kiosk selling souvenirs was said to keep medicines too. We found her.

"Have you any nose drops?"

"Yes, but not here. I've got some at home. If you'll come back in an hour's time . . ."

Dusk was falling and the air growing colder. We went into a little café to have a lemon *pisco* and a chat with José and Manuel.

"What are you doing tomorrow?" I asked them.

"Nothing. We wanted to go to the Island of the Sun, but it takes six hours each way in one of these sailing boats. And that's with a good wind. Otherwise it may be as much as eight. We'd really need two days for it, and we can't spare that much time. We have to be getting on."

"Would you like to come with us? We've got a motor-boat, and it's quite big enough for us all."

They jumped at the offer.

"You've got a wonderful aerial on your jeep."

"Yes. We've got a transmitting set."

"Don't the customs people object?"

"We don't cry it from the housetops. Particularly coming out of the Argentine. The authorities there are rather sensitive. . . . We were lucky. The customs didn't notice anything."

Our curiosity was far from satisfied. We didn't like to ask point-blank why they wanted it, however, and they never told us.

Leaving the café we went back to the kiosk. The woman drew me aside.

"They've just brought them. How many do you want?"

"A small bottle."

"No. How many drops?"

"Five in each nostril," I answered without flinching, and I made no objection when she insisted on administering them herself.

On the way back to the hotel I said:

"It's really a very good idea. To sell them drop by drop, I mean. That way, travellers don't get encumbered with bottles. I ought to have asked her to fill my fountain pen."

After dinner, we asked the lieutenant to join us in a *pisco*. Manuel and José sang us songs, accompanying themselves on the piano. We arranged to meet at three next morning.

·   ·   ·   ·   ·

E

We were all ready on time. So was breakfast, served by the proprietress of the hotel in her dressing-gown. So was the boat and the two soldiers, who had with them the bailiff of the *finca* on whose land stood the Palace of the Incas.

What with the cold and our short night, we spent the first hour huddled in the bottom of the boat, dozing. Then the sun rose, streaking the distant shores with mirages.

The navigation was done with the aid of landmarks on the shore and on the islands. There were dangers to avoid. We passed through a gap in a wall of rock, on the other side of which was the Island of the Moon or *Isla de la Luna*, whose green slopes present a much gentler landscape than does the Island of the Sun.

When we got to the latter, we saw, behind the rocks of a little creek, a domed building, which the boatmen told us was an ancient Inca fort. On landing we began painfully to climb up to it. It was worth the effort, being in an excellent state of preservation, the vaults inside intact, and we stood admiring the architectural knowledge and skill of the former masters of the lake.

The vaulting was in the shape of the corolla of a lily inverted.

"What a pity there's not enough light for a photograph," sighed Jean-Luc. "That ceiling's a marvel of workmanship."

We all of us made discoveries and called to one another to come and admire what we'd found.

Outside, one of the boatmen pointed out a path.

"Do you see that? It would take you right across the island to the Incas' palace, which you're going to see."

"We'd much rather go by boat," I said promptly. "We've done enough climbing already."

We went down to the creek where the boat was waiting, and once again we were gliding through the water, at the bottom of which we could see the pale sand.

"How shallow it is!"

"Don't you believe it. It's the clearness of the water that makes you think so. We're in more than five fathoms of water here."

On the way round, we landed on a crescent-shaped beach at the foot of a steep flight of steps, a relic of Inca days. At the base of the balusters was a channel down which ran a little stream of water, icy cold and crystal clear. Above, spurting out of the rock through conduits of Inca date, three jets of water fed the irrigated land which still surrounded the steps.

In contrast to the rest of the island the vicinity of the steps was thick with vegetation. Bushes, flowers, and eucalyptus trees reinforced the impression of abundant life given by the spurting water. We went up the steps, and I complained once again of the effort required.

Before leaving the spot, we quenched our thirst with the limpid water, for the lake water, rich in sodium sulphate, was best avoided. Presently, at the bottom of a bay, we saw the *finca* where we were to have lunch. We landed this time at a jetty. The adobe buildings here were different in colour from those we were familiar with on the plateau—of a deeper hue, orange under the bright sun.

There was a rectangular farmyard, the house forming one side. An external staircase took us up to the first floor, where a wooden balcony encircled the building. Our early start and the keen air had made us very hungry. We had lunch, then started to walk to the Palace of the Incas.

"How long will it take us to get there?" we had asked the bailiff of the *finca*.

"Half an hour. Three-quarters at the most."

It took us two whole hours. A long, rough, hilly track winding in and out among the quarries from which the stone for the palace had come. Before reaching the ruins, we came to an enormous stone beside the track. It had been part of a sanctuary remorselessly destroyed by the Spaniards. Most likely it had been an altar dedicated to the Sun-God.

Nor had the palace itself escaped the ravages of the conquerors. We felt a little cheated at having come so far to be confronted by a mere pile of stones. But the landscape was incomparable, and we could sympathize with the Emperors' choice of this site. Built on a ridge at a point where the island is very narrow, it dominated the lake, which stretched for miles on either hand.

As we climbed further along the ridge, the general plan of the palace became clear to us. The passages were narrow and winding, skirting rooms and often doubling back almost to where they had started from.

"One might almost take it for a maze," Jean-Luc remarked. "Perhaps that was the idea—to confuse the enemy and facilitate flight."

"I can't think of any other explanation."

Going down again, we walked on the walls which surrounded the whole palace.

"Really, there's not much left," I said, surveying the ruins.

"The Spaniards were at their worst here," was the answer. "The thing is, they were after hidden treasure, so they left nothing standing."

We were becoming accustomed to the Bolivians' constant and bitter complaints of the conquerors. At Machu-Pichu someone was to say to us:

"Everything's still intact. You see, the Spaniards didn't come here."

But it came as quite a surprise to us when, surveying those ruins, we suddenly heard a Bolivian say:

"What a pity it is that South America wasn't conquered by the French or the English!"

Each nation deludes itself concerning the sentiments of its subjects, or former subjects. Spain is no exception.

.   .   .   .   .

The sun was lower when we left the *finca* and said good-bye to the Island of the Sun. As we returned to Copacabana the water changed colour every minute taking on a glaucous hue which, the boatman said, might well presage a storm.

A friend in La Paz had already told us of the storms on the lake.

"The wind gets up at dusk, a little breeze which seems to have no harm in it. And then, before you know where you are, it's a gale. Enormous waves seem to come at you from every side at once. And many a boat, failing to reach shelter in time, is never seen again."

We thought about those words, not altogether assured and yet half wanting to see what a storm on the lake was like.

The sun sank over the edge of the lake, setting the whole sky ablaze. And then night fell abruptly. The lights of Copacabana went on. The cold gripped us, froze us.

The storm hadn't come after all. We were approaching the harbour now, skirting a line of rocks which in the darkness assumed fantastic shapes. One of them looked like a Virgin and Child. The wind and rain had thus fashioned it no doubt to guard the port and comfort sailors in distress.

VI

The Beni

WE had left Copacabana promising to return in August for the
Feast of the Virgin. Back in La Paz, we decided to stay there no
longer than was necessary to arrange another trip. We wanted to visit
the Potosi region to have a look at the Quechuas, and also the Sorata
region to see some more Aymara communities.

Land Reform was in full swing, creating not a little anxiety in the
capital. Wherever we went we heard of unrest in the provinces, sometimes of actual risings. We listened sceptically. Unfortunately, the
authorities who could provide us with transport couldn't be persuaded to look at things as calmly as we did.

We were sent from one department to another. We lost much
precious time in useless *démarches*. The prospect was beginning to
look hopeless when an official in the Ministry of National Education
told us that military aircraft sometimes took passengers.

We hadn't much hope, and at first our reception at the Air Force
headquarters was much the same as hitherto—we were up against
stone walls, or else officials who, shirking responsibility, passed us on
to someone else. Still we plodded on, finally reaching the top floor
which also housed the summit of rank.

"The Commander-in-Chief of the Air Force," asked Aramayo.

"I'm afraid he's away. He won't be back till Monday."

Our last hope was fading.

"Could we see his assistant?"

"Certainly. I'll tell the colonel you're here."

The colonel received us at once. After looking at our letters of
recommendation (including the Archbishop's) and listening politely
to the tale we had so often repeated, he said:

"I'm sorry I can't help you. It's quite true that military aircraft
sometimes take passengers who are eligible—and none could be more
eligible than you—but I haven't got any plane going where you want
to go. Not, that is, in the immediate future."

He called for a list and studied it.

"There's one going to Potosi in a month. You don't want to wait
that long, do you?"

He thought for a moment, then smiled.

"Would you like to take a plane at six tomorrow morning for the Beni? You won't be wasting your time, and you can be back within four days."

Somewhat taken aback, we turned to Aramayo for advice. Within five minutes we had accepted the offer and received instructions about whom we should report to at the airfield.

We had heard a good deal about the Beni from Baronne Fain, former French ambassadress at La Paz. It is a vast region of forest and pampas, traversed by the river of that name, situated in the north of Bolivia and stretching to the Matto Grosso frontier of Brazil.

It seemed funny to be taking an aeroplane to travel downwards. La Paz is twelve thousand feet up, our destination six hundred.

.   .   .   .   .

The following morning we gathered at the military aerodrome of La Paz. The cold was bitter. The wind blew right through our leather jerkins and drove clouds of Altiplano dust along the ground. The building was closed when we arrived and we stamped up and down to keep warm. The dawn began to shimmer on the snowy heights of the Ilimani.

The aerodrome was situated on the rim of the basin in which the capital lay, that is to say, it was on the edge of the Altiplano. The wind, as it whipped our cheeks, made us realize that the town was not so badly placed after all. Hitherto we had thought it strange that anyone should have wanted to build it in such a hole.

We waited and waited. The time fixed for our rendezvous was already past. The sound of an engine revving up at the civil airport made us wonder whether there had been some mistake, and we began to be seriously worried.

We were on the point of going to a hangar from which we thought we heard sounds, when a jeep dashed up, enveloping us in a swirl of dust. Out of it, to our great relief, stepped the officers we were waiting for. They took us inside to go through the final formalities.

And soon we were sitting in a row in a transport plane with our backs to the portholes.

On taking off, it headed straight for the Ilimani, climbing steadily. We were going to cross the Andes. Before long there were nothing but mountains on every side.

Passing between two snow-capped peaks we bumped violently. And then we were no longer in the dry icy air of the Altiplano, but basking in bright sunshine over a sea of fleecy clouds which seemed infinite.

Suddenly, through a gap, we had a glimpse of a dense green mass of tropical forest. Progressively the clouds thinned out as we got farther from the mountains, and finally they disappeared altogether. Then there was nothing below but forest and more forest, endless forest, the forest which sets Europeans dreaming.

We were now in the Beni country—the inhabited part of it. One of the crew came to tell us to put on our safety belts, as we were landing at Trinitad.

A primitive runway. We got out to stretch our legs. The wind was strong here, too, but as hot as that of the Altiplano had been cold. Our stop was short.

Half an hour later we landed at San Joaquim. A real tropical climate now. On the grass runway, a whole girls' school with their nun teachers had come to gape at the smart aviators.

Bordering the aerodrome, the flamboyants glowed like beacons. The flamboyant is a small tree which flowers in great yellow-centred scarlet stars. With the bougainvilia it supplies the only splash of bright colour to this tropical region.

We had a hurried meal here with the crew of the aircraft, then took off again.

Our faces glued to the portholes we stared at the forest, intersected by immense rivers. With their winding and their constant branching and rejoining it was impossible to form a clear picture of them. Sometimes we were unable to tell whether we were looking at a single *rio* or a dozen. Here and there a bare yellow patch interrupted the otherwise unbroken mass of vegetation. These were river branches which had dried out but had not yet been reconquered by the forest.

Sometimes we saw huge columns of smoke and then, as we came closer, flames. Forest fires.

At last the trees grew thinner. A small town surrounded by green fields came in sight. From above, the streets looked as if they had been drawn with a ruler. This was Riberalta, our destination, at all events for the moment.

Riberalta is a town of several thousand inhabitants. Its situation at the confluence of the Madre and the Beni has made it inevitably a commercial centre. The products of the forest are brought here, sorted out, and expedited elsewhere in large consignments. Its wealth is derived chiefly from rubber, coffee, and sweet almonds, of which three families enjoy an almost complete monopoly.

We spent two days in this town, the first of many of its type. Cool-looking, one-storeyed houses squatting by the sandy streets; quiet *patios* adorned with evergreens; hammocks hanging permanently in verandas, sometimes swollen by an indolent body swinging to and fro to create an illusion of coolness.

The hammocks are of white cotton, striped with blue, green, or red and provided with fringes to protect the sleeper from insects.

The population of the town is chiefly half-caste, with a handful of foreigners in whose hands economic power is centred. Centred for the time being, one might say, for Land Reform has not yet been proclaimed here, and no one knows what will happen when it is.

Riberalta is both a trading and financial centre. Chinese merchants somnolently wait for custom behind their counters in the shops round the square, and they can be sure their waiting won't be in vain for they stock all the things which are indispensable to forest dwellers.

The evening of our arrival we met all the leading lights of the town at the Social Club. The profit motive seems to lose its driving force in the indolence of the paradisiac climate, but it still exists, all the same. Here the interest of the big business men from abroad is in the wild *hevea* latex which, transformed into motor tyres, will one day be rolling along the highways of the United States or Europe.

Before leaving Riberalta we met the American missionaries there, and, in particular, their bishop. We had soon realized that they were very firmly established here. One could hardly go out without seeing nuns, many of them driving jeeps, which, by the way, were practically the only cars in Riberalta.

The day after our arrival we went to their headquarters on the outskirts of the town, standing by the Rio Madre or Madre de Dios. The buildings erected by the missionaries formed quite a quarter of their own, and one which breathed prosperity, if not wealth. The bishop's palace, which also housed the monks and nuns, and the hospital under construction, a little farther on, were the only buildings to have more than one storey.

At the entrance to the bishop's palace, a young man was chatting with one of the sisters. He wore light trousers and his tailless shirt hung outside them. This American looked much like his compatriots who go as students to Paris, but it was surprising to see a jewelled ring on his finger. Such femininity seemed hardly to go with pioneer work in the backwoods.

We were mistaken, however. It was no femininity at all but his badge of office. This was the bishop in person. We had already heard he was young, but had pictured a young bishop, not a young man. He received us in very friendly fashion and asked us to come and have lunch with him another day. We had to answer noncommittally, uncertain how long we should be staying.

Colonel Nogales, Governor of two districts, the Beni and the Mando, had sent us an invitation to lunch, and returning to the centre of the town we presented ourselves at his residence.

Our host, a big genial man, received us in a drawing-room. A person of considerable importance, he had at one time been Minister of the Interior. Here he lived a bachelor life, having left his wife at La Paz, owing to her inability to stand the tropical climate.

We were served with a lemon *pisco*, and were soon on easy terms. The Colonel had already inspected our 'credentials'.

"What can I do for you?"

"You can advise us how best to spend our time," I answered. "We've three days before the plane returns to La Paz."

"Not enough. You must stay longer than that. Let the plane go. There'll be another. Trust me."

We told him we trusted him implicitly.

"If you like," he suggested, "I'll lend you my *lancha* to take you up the Beni to San Pedro de Sonnenschein. I can supply the petrol; moreover, I can let you have a couple of soldiers to man the boat and act as guides. If you like the idea, you can start tomorrow morning."

This journey which hadn't been on our programme was providing some pleasant surprises. We accepted the offer with alacrity and by the time we sat down to lunch the Colonel had already given the necessary instructions.

By the middle of the afternoon our party had been augmented by two others, the regional Director of Education and his paymaster. Hearing of our trip, they had decided to take advantage of it to call on the few schoolmasters of the district.

So at dawn next morning we were all assembled in the main square of Riberalta, all, that is, except the paymaster who had evidently overslept.

"He can join us at the third bend in the river," said the Director of Education, whose name was Molinero. "It's not far to walk."

"We'd better send word to him that we've gone."

That was done, and we went down to the boat, which the two Indian soldiers were already getting ready.

The *lancha*, a six-metre decked-in boat with a small cabin aft, plodded upstream slowly, though the stream was not rapid. Indeed the Beni we found to be a sluggish, muddy river, thick with the earth it had washed away from its banks. The water was low at that season, and the high banks were often overhanging, though still supporting trees. Leaning out over the water, these were obviously destined to fall in sooner or later, their trunks being added to the innumerable others which already encumbered the *rio*.

"*Palo, palo,*" cry the boatmen when a log is sighted ahead.

The Beni is five or six times the width of the Seine at Paris. It twists and turns unceasingly as it meanders lazily through the forest.

Our boatmen, the Indian soldiers, kept crossing the river so as to take advantage of the shorter distance and slacker water on the inside of the bends. Gradually we learnt to estimate the depth of the river from the colour of the water. On the whole this wide river is shallow.

One of our guides said:

"By the Beni there are lots of lakes swarming with caymans and piranhas. You'll see presently."

Like all the tributaries of the Amazon, the Beni is flanked by virgin forest, immense, impenetrable, and full of cries. Indeed, in it one hears much more than one sees.

The river of course attracts many animals. Egrets hunt for food along the banks. Flights of parrots and parakeets mix their vivid colours with the dark green of the trees.

On fallen trunks we saw giant tortoises basking in the sun, and nine-foot-long lizards doing the same on the banks of the little side-streams. The caymans, which grow to the same length, remained absolutely motionless till the noise of the *lancha's* motor dragged them from their sleep. Then with a 'plop' they disappeared, their tails leaving a track in the soft alluvial soil.

Now and again we saw an Indian hamlet, or *baraca*. Passing an island, we asked its name.

"The Lepers' Island," came the answer.

We should have liked to stop, but our guides didn't take to the idea. The island is used as a refuge on which a few lepers are isolated.

"The *lancha's* too heavy," said the boatmen. "If we don't push on, we'll never make the distance."

We were indeed making very poor progress. We should have reached our first port of call, Yvon, by noon. It now seemed doubtful whether we should be there by nightfall. We were told, moreover, that the river was dangerous at night because of the floating tree-trunks.

At half-past five we had not yet arrived, and we knew that in that latitude it would be quite dark in another half-hour.

The guides suggested making fast to the bank for the night and sleeping in the boat. We talked to each other in French, pretending not to understand them, and when darkness came we still chugged on, dangerous as it certainly was. It was hard enough to spot the floating trunks in daylight; quite impossible now. The south wind, or *surazo*, which had risen, seemed bitterly cold after the heat of the day. The temperature couldn't have been far below seventy degrees Fahrenheit, yet it drove right through us, chilling us to the marrow. To keep it out we rolled ourselves in our hammocks, toga fashion, which gave us somewhat the appearance of ancient Romans on the Tiber.

A quarter of an hour went by, then another, then another. Our guides were still talking of tying up for the night.

Suddenly a light shone through the trees. The helmsman's face lit up.

"Yvon."

Yvon was merely a trading station, belonging to the Suarez family, who had formerly been the greatest landowners in all Bolivia.

Everyone sighed with relief. It didn't take us long to come abreast of it. We jumped ashore and climbed up the steep river bank, tripping every second or two over a root or a branch.

The house and its outbuildings were walled in. Three watch-dogs showed their teeth threateningly, but they had already performed their duty in announcing our presence, and a man came to let us in.

It was the manager, and once again we were given a most friendly reception and put up for the night.

The following day, when we mentioned the weight and slowness of the Colonel's *lancha*, we were offered a much lighter boat (this one called a *casco*) to which it was quite a simple matter to transfer the *lancha's* outboard motor. The difference in speed was considerable. Having tried it out we decided, against the weight of opinion, to continue our journey at once.

"The day's too far gone now. We may not reach any place and be obliged to spend the night in the open."

"Never mind. At a pinch we can always sling our hammocks between two trees. Besides, there's every chance of finding a *baraca*."

There was a long argument in the course of which our two pilots were won over. We pushed off.

They regretted having sided with us, however, as darkness was soon upon us. It was night when we arrived at Pékin, where we found a half-caste delighted to take us in. Once again the *surazo* had started blowing at sunset, and the *casco* had provided even less shelter from it than the *lancha*.

We had stopped at the mouth of a small tributary which, at the moment, had hardly any water in it. The mud made it difficult to land till the Indians rolled some logs down, on which we could step ashore quite easily. We were taken along a path through the forest to a little clearing in which there were three houses of the type usually described as bamboo huts.

Stakes driven into the ground made the four corners. The roof was a sort of thatch of dried palm leaves, the walls of stems of the *palma brava*, a small wild palm tree about eighteen feet high, whose slender stems are no more than an inch and a half in diameter. We were told that the first settlers here, who were Japanese, used to eat the pith. And indeed the pith of some palm trees cut young (about two years old) is delicious to eat, either cooked or cold as a salad. The name varies. In some regions it is called *palmito*, in others *chonta*. In taste it is not unlike asparagus or globe artichoke, but in our opinion more delicate.

To make walls, the *palma brava* is cut to the desired length and the stems fastened side by side, the interstices being left open so that air can pass freely.

The same material is used underfoot, the stems being in this case plaited to make a very springy floor, which rests on battens about fifteen inches from the ground, out of reach of the various forms of animal life which could make themselves disagreeable.

Our host's wife appeared in the doorway and called us in to dinner. She took us into a low hut opposite, which did duty both as kitchen and dining-room. The floor here was simply beaten earth. A fire burnt in a corner, the smoke going up through the roof.

Having eaten we slung our hammocks in the house, while our host retired to the room he occupied with his family. As we settled down, vampire bats kept flying through the room, in at one door and out at another. They are huge creatures which suck the blood of poultry and cattle. They fly as noiselessly as our bats and with equal precision, never bumping into anything, though moving at great speed.

"You see, they're fitted with a sort of radar," Jean-Luc informed us.

"They need it. They're practically blind."

"I once knew a man," I said, "who used to go in for bat-shooting. That takes some doing as they zigzag all the time."

"But is it true that vampire bats sometimes attack humans?" one of us asked.

"Rarely grown-ups, though they have been known to go for a sleeping man. They prick his big toe, hovering over it, their wings beating all the time. That's how the legend has arisen that they 'put the sleeper to sleep' by fanning him."

They do quite often attack children when they find them sleeping in hammocks. They can easily get at their victim through the mesh of the net. We had seen traces of blood on hammocks hanging in the *baracas* and on one occasion a boy with a large bloodstain on the shoulder of his short.

"They often go for the shoulders," we were told. "It's the most accessible part of a body lying in a hammock."

We slept under mosquito-netting, as the cold hadn't chased the insects away.

With insufficient blankets we shivered in our hammocks, as the wind came right through the walls.

Finally I got up and put on four shirts, one on top of the other.

"Are you asleep, Aramayo?" asked Jean-Luc.

"No. It's too cold. And the mosquitoes are biting me right through my hammock. It would be better to get up and go for a walk."

But I promptly went to sleep, only to wake up again a little later. The cold gave me gooseflesh. I got up and walked about for a while outside. Then, finding a sack lying about, decidedly damp and by no means scrupulously clean, I brought it in and lined my hammock with it to keep the wind out.

Next morning at dawn we were drinking coffee, scalding hot and extremely comforting.

"How did you manage to sleep so well in the end, Bernard?"

"What with my four shirts and the old sack, I was almost warm."

"And the mosquitoes?"

"They never bite me, neither here nor in France."

Aramayo made a remark about some people having thick skins.

Going down to the *rio* we found it was still too early to start. Hanging three feet above the surface of the water was a sheet of fog, the result of the cold during the night.

We hadn't long to wait, however. As it rose, the sun swept the fog away in no time.

Soon the heat was oppressive, and the glare of the sun, reflected by the water, was painful to the eyes.

On we went, upstream, between sandy banks. We acquired a growing respect for our boatmen, whose eyesight was phenomenal.

We discussed at some length the sharpness of eye of the Indians.

"It's only because they're familiar with the scene," maintained Jean-Luc.

"Admittedly they are," I answered, "but that's not enough to explain it. When they point to something ahead, it's another ten minutes before we see it, and then only as the minutest dot."

Arguing, we whiled away the time.

I was sitting in the bow with my loaded gun resting on the gunwale, Jean-Luc aft with the camera. Aramayo had a gun too.

I have shooting in the blood and each bird was a novelty for me; I shot right and left at grey egrets, white egrets and *pajaro bobos*. The latter, whose name means 'silly bird', reminded us, both in gait and colour, of a woman we had met in La Paz.

.   .   .   .   .

It is quite impossible to say what distance we travelled. The *rios* are deceptive, and the boatmen calculated only in hours, and then with glaring inexactitude.

Above Pékin, the *baracas* became rarer. But, as the human population thinned out, the animal population increased. Alligators and tortoises were abundant. Big toucans, blue and red, flew from one bank of the river to the other, while white and grey egrets perched on the branches.

Seeing a sleeping cayman on the opposite bank, we steered towards it, stopping the engine so as to make no noise. When we had drifted as far as the way of the boat would take us, Aramayo fired, but missed, and we heard once again the 'plop' as the creature dived.

On we went. The heat was suffocating and we couldn't remove our sun-helmets. The tepid water of the *rio* was quite unable to quench our thirst, merely leaving a little mud in our mouths.

Suddenly on the left bank we saw a *baraca*, high up above us, for the bank was very steep here. It was surrounded by trees, oranges amongst them. We asked the boatmen to stop so that we could buy some.

It was a paradisiac spot. Five or six boys, all but naked, came running down towards us, while at the top of the path stood a wrinkled old woman and a few young men.

"Can you sell us some oranges?"

The old thing went off readily to pick some, though she had been warned she mustn't charge us much. While she was away, we walked round the house, scaring the pigs and chickens who had taken advantage of their mistress's absence to have a peep indoors.

"Have you ever eaten coffee berries?" asked Aramayo.

We picked some and tried to define the taste.

"Red currant."

"What's that tree with the large green fruit?" I asked.

"A *calabasero* (calabash). The gourds are cut in two and left to dry."

The old Indian woman returned carrying, to our great surprise, a huge basket of more than a hundred and fifty oranges.

We gobbled some of them then and there, after which we went down to the *casco* again, sending the two soldiers up to fetch the basket.

Perhaps Jean-Luc had been right after all: our eyes were getting rapidly used to looking into the distance. We had already noticed a yellow roof, when our two Indians cried out:

"*Los salvajes!*"

The savages. Soon other huts came into sight and we saw people making off hurriedly into the forest.

We landed as quickly as we could and went up to the settlement. The huts were different from any we had seen so far. Four stakes held up a low roof made of dried grass of a vivid yellow. The palm leaf roofs of that region take on with time a characteristic grey colour.

But what was most strange was the lowness of the roofs. We had never seen anything like it. These huts seemed to have been made for pygmies, yet the people we had seen running away had been of normal stature.

It was obvious the 'savages' hadn't been there long. The *chacra* was recent. A *chacra* is a clearing (made by burning down the trees) which is subsequently cultivated. When the land is exhausted, the settlers move on. The forest takes back its own, temporarily at least, for they may come back to the same spot some years later.

Half-burnt stumps of trees were visible between the banana trees. A dense thicket of sugar cane hid some of the natives who were taking cover. We heard raucous sounds coming from it and other cries coming from the forest.

Beyond the banana trees, however, we managed to find a few people, some scantily dressed women and a man who spoke a little Spanish and was able to give us some information.

The little community belonged to a tribe of the Chamas. The Chamas are to be met all over the Western areas of the Amazon basin. They are noted for their pottery, particularly for their white-necked jars decorated with black geometrical designs. The ones here had come from an affluent a long way upstream. One of them had not only seduced another man's wife but had killed the man (who had raised objections). This domestic drama had split the tribe in two, and one part had moved off, wandering down the banks of the Beni.

In general the Chamas had a rather bad reputation in the region, but we found them very friendly. As soon as they were convinced we hadn't come to round up young men for military service, they showed us every hospitality.

We wanted some special oil which was said to be very good for the hair. When we enquired, they said they had some and gave it us most readily. The difficult thing was to pay them for it. They knew that money existed, but had not the faintest idea of the value of our notes. We gave them a hundred bolivianos (about a shilling), but if we had given them a hundredth part of that, it would have been just the same to them.

Aramayo warned us not to put anything down, as a Chama would snatch it straight away. This habit probably dates from the first contacts with the whites, the native picking up and appropriating anything which the white man threw away.

Most of the women were painted. The oldest of those around us had her arms and legs painted with fish-bone patterns.

The huts were all alike. In one of them a newborn baby was sleeping amongst a lot of half-finished pottery. Round each hut ran a strip of plaited palm leaves to keep out the wind and the sun.

We left with regret, promising to come back again, bringing with us what they were most in need of—ammunition for their guns.

Our next and final stop was to be San Pedro. We hadn't petrol enough to go further. The heat was more oppressive than ever and we longed to reach our destination. We had come to mistrust our boatmen's sense of time and distance. It was always:

"Another hour."

Or:

"Round two more bends."

Finally they couldn't help being right. Another hour, two more bends, and the river stopped winding, stretching out ahead of us in a long straight line. The forest seemed to recede, or perhaps the trees

Funeral cortège running across the Altiplano

The Island of the Sun. View from ruins of the Incas' Palace

The old Uru sent by God

were not so tall. Our companions told us that the screen of *palma brava* on one side of the river marked the first plantation of rubber trees in Bolivia. So far we had only come across the wild trees whose latex was collected by the *seringueros*.

A *seringuero* is generally a half-caste. He fights his way through the dense virgin forest, hacking a path from one tree to the next. To keep the path cleared is an almost daily struggle. In no time, if given a chance, the forest will close in and swallow it up.

At first we could see no signs of life. Then a solitary house appeared which we were told was a school. More *palma brava*, then a long grassy stretch, on which we landed. We had reached San Pedro de Sonnenschein at last.

The next day Jean-Luc went off to inspect the rubber plantation, while I preferred to go fishing and shooting with the younger of the two soldiers.

Taking the *casco* we crossed to the other side of the Beni, our objective being a lake hidden in the forest. Making the boat fast, we plunged into the dense mass of vegetation. There was a path, but it was already overgrown since it had last been used, and we had to hack our way through with the aid of a *machete*.

It took a little time for one's eyes to get used to the darkness of the forest. There were plenty of sounds, mysterious and disquieting rustlings, but nothing visible. The immensely tall trees, the tangle of lianas and aerial roots completely obliterated the sun, allowing nothing below but a deep glaucous shadow, in which a certain physical discomfort reinforced an unreasoning anxiety.

High overhead, near the young philodendron shoots hung the sumptuous orchids, but one guessed their presence rather than saw them.

Presently we left the path for an even less beaten track, along which we had to clamber over enormous tree trunks or crawl under half-rotted branches.

Suddenly I stopped dead in my tracks, grasping my gun. A formidable noise on my right seemed as though it could only herald a stampede of fifty wild boars. But it stopped as suddenly as it had started. Reassured but disappointed, I saw the Indian smile.

"What's the matter?" he asked.

"Hush. There must be animals about."

"Oh no. It's only a bird, and quite a small one, making the leaves flutter as it flew off."

F

A minute or two later he said:

"Here we are. Here's the lake."

Just before reaching it we saw strewn on the ground the red and blue feathers of a toucan, victim of a bird of prey.

Between their branches and the twining lianas, a vague scintillation showed where the lake was. We hacked our way through, reaching it at a place where a forked tree overhung the water. Climbing into the fork, I was able to survey the lake, which, from its shape and size, was obviously a former bend in the Rio Beni that had been pinched off.

The Indian, who had followed me into the tree, pointed out a bird standing on a narrow beach.

"Kill it."

I took aim and fired. The bird floundered by the edge of the water.

We ran towards it. When it saw us, the bird raised its beak menacingly. It was a bird of prey and looked dangerous. When it opened its wings, the Indian recoiled.

"I'd better finish it off," I said, raising my gun again.

When it was dead the Indian picked it up. It was a big black bird, the spread of whose wings was nearly five feet. The white claws which had scared the man were spiny processes growing from the joints of the wings, the longest of them being nearly two inches. Not only were their points very sharp but their edges cut like razors.

"You see," said the Indian, "it folds its prey in its wings. Those spikes are deadly. Afterwards it uses its beak. . . . Lend me your knife. I'll cut a bit of its flesh for bait."

Plunging the blade between the feathers, he cut some slices. The flesh was deep red; some blood dripped from the knife. The soldier laughed and gave me a friendly look. The laugh turned to a smile as he wiped the blade and plunged it into the earth to clean it.

"Good knife. Good for killing man," he observed with satisfaction, and, throwing it, he speared a tree.

From his pocket he produced his somewhat elementary fishing tackle, a line with a hook on the end. Retrieving the knife, he cut the flesh into small cubes, with one of which he baited the hook. He coiled the line, held the coil in his right hand, and with the left threw the end with the hook as far as he could into the lake. There was just time for a ripple to form and a fish bit at once. But the man jerked the line too late; when he hauled it in, there was nothing on the hook.

"Not quick enough. Not hard enough," he said.

Next time he was luckier and landed a piranha about four inches long. The piranha is in general shape much like the perch of our rivers. The jaws look like saws, the teeth of which interlock. It was easy to understand how the Indians came to use them as knives and even sometimes as arrow-heads.

The man cut a forked stick and impaled the fish.

He went on, and before long needed another stick to hold his catch, the largest of which was about ten inches long. His eyes sparkled with pleasure.

The fish bit instantly, but they were apt to let go almost as promptly, so he had to be very quick.

"Look at their teeth. But mind out for your fingers. Use your knife."

I did as I was bid. As soon as they felt the blade of the knife, the piranhas bit savagely. It took hours for them to die.

"Try with a stick."

I thrust a stick in the mouth of one. It was impossible to pull it out again. When I lifted the stick up, the fish came too, refusing to let go.

"I can see why you were anxious about my fingers."

The Indian answered with a laugh.

"I think that's enough. Shall we go and see if there is anything to shoot?"

"Right."

He led the way along the winding path, saying little, his movements quiet as a cat's. Suddenly he turned to me.

"There's a man there."

"Where?"

"Over there."

But I could see nothing but the trees. A moment later, however, I saw a rubber tree whose trunk was marked with slanting cuts, from the lowest of which oozed a white liquid like skimmed milk, which dripped into a rusty tin.

The soldier turned round again to whisper:

"This is a *seringuero's* path. The man I saw must have been collecting latex. Gently now! We'd better make sure."

Obediently, I endeavoured to move as quietly as my guide, avoiding the dead twigs that might crackle underfoot.

"Just like duck-shooting," I thought.

The Indian stopped again.

"Yes. It's a *seringuero* all right. Do you see his can?"

Rather like a milk can. Into it was poured the latex he collected.

What beat me was how the Indian had spotted the man in the dense vegetation.

The *seringuero* turned out to be a small, young Indian with huge, brilliant eyes which devoured his face. He spoke little Spanish, in fact he seemed to have more use for his legs than for his tongue. That was not surprising, however. To go from rubber tree to rubber tree the whole day long collecting latex is certainly a solitary occupation. I was conscious of a profound shyness in him.

He pointed in the direction in which we might find two Indian *canoas* on the lake. The next moment his sky-blue cap was lost in the forest.

I once more followed my Indian guide, who presently struck off from the path to cut a way through the undergrowth. Winding this way and that he yet kept a perfect sense of direction, and we came out on the lake exactly where the two *canoas* were tied up.

Before that, when still in the thick of the forest, the Indian had stopped and asked me to lend him my gun to shoot a pigeon. How he could see a pigeon in that tangle of leaves and branches was a mystery. Looking over his shoulder, I could see no sign of it. Only after the shot had been fired did I see the bird fall.

The *canoas* were apparently quite unusable, being completely immersed in the water. When he saw them the Indian groaned, then, brightening, he asked me to help him.

While I lifted one of them, the Indian baled out with his cupped hands. Presently the *canoa* was empty. It was a typical specimen, made out of a tree trunk, the interior burnt out, the exterior trimmed with a *machete*.

The Indian examined the bottom and sides, and with damp earth caulked any cracks he could find. When satisfied with his work, he looked around for a paddle and found one in the bushes.

I crouched with my gun, while the other paddled.

"Are you all ready to shoot? There are lots of caymans here. They can't hear us in this craft. It's not like the *casco* with the motor."

We swept round in a wide circle, but without seeing a thing. In spite of the caulking, the *canoa* leaked, and in any case it was time to think of getting back.

Returning the *canoa* to its place, we walked back to the river, found the *casco* and were soon cruising along the opposite bank of the river.

"There! See that iguana? Shoot it. Be quick or it'll dive."

It was a fine specimen nearly five feet long which I took proudly back to San Pedro. Jean-Luc, who had long been back, photographed it. The remarkable thing was its power of changing colour, which it retained long after death. On the grass it turned green, and a little later, on the kitchen tiles, red.

It was now time to leave San Pedro. The journey back to Riberalta was accomplished much more speedily of course, since we were going downstream. It was uneventful, save that we nearly ran out of petrol before the end. For some distance we drifted, keeping what little was left for crossing the mouth of the Madre, which was known to be dangerous owing to the presence of many tree trunks, and all the more so since we were arriving in the dark.

.   .   .   .   .

On arrival we had a hasty dinner, after which Jean-Luc went straight to bed, while Aramayo and I wandered round the little town. There was some sort of a *fiesta* on, but the only signs of it were a few gambling tables in a blaze of electric light near the bishop's palace.

"I won't try my luck," I said, "but I'd enjoy watching you."

"Don't you like gambling?"

"Only too well! I'd much better leave it alone, though I generally have marvellous luck. Do people gamble much in Bolivia?"

"Terribly. I can give you an example. A certain colonel belonging to a rich family was gambling. First he lost all the money he had on him, then, on his word of honour, the whole of his fortune. Finally his house. Even then he wouldn't stop. Having nothing else to offer, he pledged his wife. He lost her too. Arriving at the colonel's house, the winner said: '*Señora*, this house is now mine. So for that matter are you, but, though I have won you, I shall merely ask you to go.'"

The place was very animated, crowds pressing round the tables, which were covered with green cloths chalked out in squares. Without attempting to understand what was going on, I moved from table to table surveying the scene. Aramayo, on the other hand, was completely lost in the game. He won, he lost, won again, and finally came away a little poorer than he had started.

"No need to mention it to my wife," he said, as we sat in an improvised café over a glass of beer.

The next day we learnt that there wouldn't be a plane for La Paz for several days.

We decided to go to Guayaramerin, where we thought we had

more chance of finding one. Between Riberalta and Guayaramerin, on the Brazilian frontier, was a regular air service, and the flight only took us a quarter of an hour. On our arrival we found that getting back to La Paz was as great a problem as ever, and we decided to go up the Rio Mamore on the paddle steamer that was leaving that afternoon.

Guayaramerin, or rather the main part of it, is separated from Brazil by the Mamore, only a small part being on the Brazilian side. Being astride of a frontier it naturally favoured trafficking of every description. The currency of both countries was in circulation, the cruzeiro being somewhat less unstable than the boliviano.

On board the *Adolfo Arauz*, we slung our hammocks on the upper deck, reserved for first-class passengers. On the deck below, the second-class passengers slung theirs where they could without getting in the way of the sailors. Accompanying us was another boat with two decks on the lower of which passengers and freight were all mixed up, hammocks flying in the wind. They even slaughtered a cow there. We consumed it bit by bit during the voyage, as well as the unborn calf that was found inside.

On the other side, a third boat carried fuel for the boiler, that is to say, wood. We stopped every three hours or so to take in a fresh supply.

We travelled with the proprietor of a *hacienda* and several trades-women. In a sing-song Spanish, they discussed the cost of living and opened large suitcases to show their wares: coloured textiles, medica-ments, syringes, boxes of flowered buttons, children's clothing and, choicest treasure of all, a bunch of artificial flowers. After these had been admired by all they were stowed away in the pilot's cabin.

In a country where real flowers bloom all the year round without anyone having to bother about them, these artificial flowers struck us as decidedly bizarre.

For several days we steamed up the river accompanied by the slow rhythm of the paddles which scared away the alligators and tortoises. It would have been a lovely journey if we hadn't been obliged to eat that meat (which got higher day by day), served with boiled green bananas.

On reaching Santiago de Suarez we learnt that an aeroplane was leaving next day for La Paz. Thus ended our travels in the Beni, which had been intended to last four days, but which had in the end taken four times as long.

VII

The Feast of the Virgin

WHEN we got back to La Paz it was time to think of returning to Copacabana. On no account did we want to miss the Feast of the Virgin, the most important *fiesta* of the year in Bolivia. Yet it was far from certain that we should be able to get to it. So great was its attraction that no means of transport was available until Mr. Green, Director of the Inter-American Agricultural Service, kindly came to our rescue.

At our hotel in La Paz we had found two young men, old friends of mine, Michel Leclerc and Jean-Claude Bois, who had just returned from Alaska. They, too, were intending to go to Copacabana. They rode ahead of us on their motor scooters.

When we came to the ferry at Tiquina we found a long queue of lorries and cars waiting to cross. On both sides of the water were rows of Indian women sitting behind little tables selling beer and coffee to all comers, from members of the diplomatic corps down to the families of patiently waiting Indians.

Bearing official papers, we were given priority and crossed quite quickly.

There was an unbroken chain of vehicles all the way from Tiquina to Copacabana on the road which normally carries only an occasional flock of sheep or llamas, to say nothing of the groups of Indians who had come from great distances on foot. Many of the Indians spun as they went, drawing the wool from bags tucked under their arms. Their wives had bundles on their backs containing clothes, meagre provisions, and their sleeping babies.

At every turn in the road we were assailed by groups of beggars holding out their hands or hats, importuning us in Aymara, and only making way before the curses of our Indian chauffeur.

Copacabana was very different from the sleepy place we had visited before. The crowd was so dense that we could only advance at a walking pace, the screen of *ponchos* opening up in front of us, then closing again behind. At one point we passed a group of dancers with high-plumed head-dresses, who were playing an ancient air on the *kéna*.

87

The fiesta of Copacabana was no easy thing to organize. The frenzy of the dancing, impossible to subjugate, had nevertheless to be kept within bounds. The Prefect's speech must be decorously listened to, and the procession must not be jostled by the crowds.

There is in the Indians a latent wildness which easily kicks over the traces.

The centre of the *fiesta* was the big square in front of the church, on all sides of which Indians were selling clothes, blankets, *lluchos*, and pottery. The groups of dancers who occupied the corners and the parvis never stopped except for drink.

On the steps of the church a hundred old Indians squatting on the ground were playing violins. They took no notice of us as we stepped over them. Other Indians came up, spoke to them in low tones and touched their hands caressingly. The violin players were being given money by people who came to consult the sorcerers, now chanting prayers to the accompaniment of the instruments. Each chant expressed a wish.

It was all a very queer mixture, disconcerting at first, but we soon got used to it.

We entered the church.

Turning off from the nave we found ourselves in a sort of hall where literally thousands of candles were burning under the eyes of old crouching sorcerers who watched them to foretell the future. Each candle represented some wish or other or a person whose fate was being asked after.

"O God, make it that two and two no longer make four," said Pushkin, putting in a nutshell the majority of human prayers.

Leaving the hall of candles, we went back along the nave through the medley of sorcerers and monks, and as we went one of us said:

"I wish I was rich. I'd like to pay the Pope his travelling expenses to come and see this."

Outside, the festivities continued. On our right, a ring of onlookers stood watching dancers in silk tunics whirling round and round. Their plumed head-dresses, three feet high, were made to look like flowers. A handful of musicians played indefatigably. Suddenly the dancers would stop, have a drink, and then go on again.

Most of them were already drunk, but that didn't seem to affect their dancing. We saw one unable to walk straight who, back in the dance, performed without a fault. We asked the chief of a troop when the show would reach its climax.

"It only needs a bit more to warm up the musicians," was the answer.

A bit more to drink, naturally.

In another corner, the dancers had wigs of long black hair falling down their backs, and bands across their foreheads. They symbolized the Indians of the forest. They danced bending forward, then suddenly straightening up, accompanied by the *sampoña*, a pan-pipe made up of a number of reeds tied together with plaited straw.

It is impossible to describe the frenzy of the dance. Each face wore a different expression and struck a different note in the symphony.

Through a small door in the church another group of dancers emerged, having prayed before they got to work. They wore the Quechua *poncho*, purple with black patterns, and short trousers sewn round their thighs. Two by two they came forward to the sound of a flute, proceeding to a corner that was still unoccupied.

It wasn't easy to understand the dances or guess their origins. In search of information, I went into a grocer's shop and questioned the woman who owned it. She didn't know much about folklore, but she knew the Indians.

"They can go on like that for days and nights at a stretch. Without any sleep. Without ever seeming to get tired. Of course they drink a lot—that keeps them going, that and the coca leaves they chew all the time."

On this day the Indian frenzy burst out, bottled up during so many long months of patient toil.

Frames of various shapes and sizes—houses, pediments, hoops— were being set up to hold the evening's fireworks. In the general hubbub we could no longer hear the blasts of dynamite which, as a sign of joy, had been going off all day long in the surrounding hills.

"Tomorrow the procession. Tomorrow the procession," came the cry on all sides of us, punctuated by crackers.

Careless or even dishonest travellers have spoken of ritual combats and other cruel rites. The reality was different, but it was enough. With our friends we went everywhere filming, questioning, and trying to take part in the *fiesta* ourselves.

After dinner we went back to the main square with four Brazilians with whom we had struck up an acquaintance; one of them, half French, acted as our interpreter.

The fireworks had started. The whole place was ablaze. A small procession of priests was passing. Behind us a group of Indians, under the direction of the monks, was draping the arches of the church with streamers. Women on ladders pinned onto the stuff every bit of silver they could lay their hands on. Another group was decorating the entrance.

Rockets were fired, answered by the dynamite in the distance, the sounds floating out across the vast stretches of the lake.

The faces of the Indians were more and more extraordinary as they watched with a sort of haggard ecstasy the rockets soar into the sky.

For us, the real show wasn't the fireworks at all, but themselves, these Indians whose *fiesta* it was.

In the end we got separated by the swarming crowd, only finding each other again when we gathered finally, all four of us, in our common room. Sleep was difficult as the blasts of dynamite never stopped coming from the hills.

When we got back to the square first thing next morning, it didn't seem as if the dancers had ever stopped. Nor had they.

Near the parvis of the church, a hawker had laid his wares out on a large white cloth. Chief among them were amulets—small hands carved out of bone or stone, the fingers half closed on the palm which bore a solar emblem. These amulets bring luck. Other wares, in small linen bags, included sulphur, starfish, skeins of coloured wool, and powders of various hues. These were for use in the sacrifices made by the sorcerers in tiny little pots of doll's house dimensions, which also were on sale everywhere. As for the amulets, I had already bought some in La Paz, where a whole quarter dealt in goods of magical property.

"What's that stuff?" asked one of our friends from Alaska, pointing to a heap.

"Foetuses," answered Jean-Luc promptly. "Pigs' or llamas'. We learnt about them at Jesus de Machaca. They're always put in the foundations when a house is built. They act as a protection."

"And those bracelets of dried meat?"

The man who sold them explained that they freed children of worms.

The procession would soon be starting, so Jean-Luc wandered off in search of a suitable place in which to set up his film camera. I lined up with the crowd.

A military band was already on the church steps, waiting to head the procession.

A stir by the main door. A big statue bowed its way under the arch. It was the Virgin, greeted by a joyful shout from the crowd. She wasn't the one we had seen inside, too precious to be allowed out of the church, but she was decked out in the same style, dressed in bejewelled white, her diadem sparkling with a thousand gems. She stood on a pedestal resting on the shoulders of six men. As they advanced slowly, she pitched slightly up and down like a boat moving through a light swell. High above the crowd she moved, while all eyes were lifted towards her, and the voices of thousands of women cried out.

Surrounding the pedestal was a group of priests dressed in silver and gold, advancing majestically between the double hedge of Indians.

Crackers were fired off on all sides. The procession was about to descend the steps which divided the parvis of the church from the square. The bearers moved more slowly still, taking the utmost care of the Queen of Heaven going out to meet her people. A pole was thrust up from the middle of the delirious crowd ringed with multi-coloured rockets, from which, on bursting, floated out large Bolivian flags.

Then the procession went right round the square under a rain of confetti which fluttered down on the white dress and on the priests' brilliant chasubles. The priests, the protectors of the Indians, seemed touched by this demonstration of their faith.

Thousands of bags of confetti must have been thrown, for when the procession was over we found that the church itself was full of it.

Harmless ammunition. Other missiles were less so. At one corner of the square a veritable bombardment of oranges began. Nor was the Virgin spared. More than one caught her full in the face. One orange, bouncing off a priest's head, came to rest among a sorcerer's wares, where it lay symbolizing religion in the midst of superstition.

The crowd opened up just enough to let the procession pass, then closed again behind it. The excitement of every Indian reached its height as the statue passed close by, but it was impossible not to feel that this religious ceremony was more an outlet for their exuberance than the cause of it. It's all very well for the priests to say the Indians are Catholics; those who know them cannot escape the conviction that their religious fervour has come straight down to them from pagan times.

Needing a rest from the hullaballoo, we walked down to the lake, where of course we found nobody. The little waves of the lake lapped a deserted beach of pink and blue pebbles. Boats, with their sails furled, rocked gently. The Island of the Sun seemed plunged in an eternal sleep.

This, however, was merely a breather. The next item on the programme was the *diablada* which was to take place on a piece of ground near the port. Soon Indian men and women were wending their way there, some carrying bottles of beer to sell to the spectators.

The *diablada* is a masked dance famous in Bolivia. It really belongs to the Oruro district, but a company specializing in its performance goes round from *fiesta* to *fiesta* with this extraordinary spectacle.

Presently the dancers appeared at the top of the street walking slowly down towards us. They had already given a performance on the square, but we had had great difficulty in filming it owing to the large number of dancers and the crowd pressing round. Here in a more open space we hoped to have better luck.

We made the acquaintance of the leading dancer, who introduced us to the principal characters. They were St. Michael, Lucifer, Satan, the Seven Deadly Sins (one dancer to each sin), the Condemned, the Crafty Man, the Woman of the World.

All were masked. Of the many others, some were animals (a bear, a bull, a stag with antlers), but the majority were devils, all with horned masks and decked with bits of mirror which glittered in the sun.

The masks were enormous, out of proportion to the body.

St. Michael carried a sword and had an oval mirror as a breastplate. It was his role to fight the devils and their richly adorned chiefs, Satan and Lucifer. He always won.

But the most striking of all was the Woman of the World, who was sometimes called Temptation. The part was played by a man in woman's clothes, whose face was painted with a pale make-up to ape the complexion of a European prostitute.

The music was supplied by a small orchestra, which differed little from what you might find in any country town in France.

There were a considerable number of figures, not all of which were danced at every performance. The most important thing about the show was the indescribable exaltation of the dancers, who literally seemed possessed. Like Whirling Dervishes they could go on endlessly without tiring.

The performance over, one of the dancers went round collecting money, which was then shared out and spent on drink.

We managed to take a film, the only trouble being that the performers wanted to see the result immediately. It was only by putting up more money for drink that we got them to leave us in peace.

Returning to the square, we noticed a group of dancers we had not yet seen. They were called the *luchabotes* or the *chunchus*, and their dance the *sicuriada*. Many of these dancers were masked too. Those who were not had brightly painted faces. The costumes were those of the Indians of the forest with feathers worked into the hair. There were more devils, but with simpler masks than those of the *diablada*, the horns shorter. Animals too—stags, iguanas, and a white horse wearing a top hat with a red-white-and-blue ribbon. Other dancers had long red tunics hanging over their blue trousers. The stags in particular interested me, not that I had any idea of taking a pot-shot at them, but because I knew that this animal played an important part in the purification rites celebrated after hunting by Indians in both North and South America.

In some tribes the hunter, after eating the meat, has to put the bones back in the hide and bury them. We had actually seen this custom applied to a llama at Jesus de Machaca.

The iguana mask was terrifying. We recognized it at once from the iguana I had shot on the Rio Beni.

Unlike those of the *diablada*, these dancers accompanied themselves, using pan-pipes and drums. They went round and round, one behind the other. Sometimes they stopped suddenly, but only to turn and go round the other way.

Later, one of us went into the church, which was deserted. The silver trinkets still glittered on the brown drapery. After a moment a group of dancers with enormous drums strapped to their chests entered by another door.

In the silence of the church the murmur of the crowd outside was audible and sometimes, quite distinctly, the rhythm of a dance. Occasionally the noise of the crowd would subside as they listened to a solo singer.

Flutes struck up on the parvis. A priest appeared and intoned some words in Latin. Then the music died down, and the dancers in the church beat their enormous drums. When they stopped, the flutes started again. This alternation was repeated three or four times. Then the dancers backed out of the church, but came in again before disappearing finally.

The *fiesta* came to an end. We had to get back to La Paz. In the early hours of the morning we succeeded in boarding a *gondola* though it was already crammed with people.

At Tiquina, after crossing in the ferry, we found a spectacle awaiting us. At some distance from each other, two groups of dancers were executing figures. Their costumes were quite different from any we had seen so far. One group wore red and yellow head-dresses from which hung white and gold beads. In the midst of them a man was dancing in a miner's helmet.

The others were dressed in a simple blue costume with necklaces of shells. They carried bows, arrows, and agricultural implements.

The first represented the new Indians, the second the original inhabitants of the region. Presently they approached each other, held off, then finally merged in a single dance, symbolizing the fusion of new and old in a common tradition.

VIII

Potosi

THE train rumbled over the Altiplano. We had left in the morning to visit the mines at Potosi, called Imperial after the Emperor Charles V, who was Charles I of Spain. We intended also to study the agrarian communities in the neighbourhood.

Aramayo was with us again. He had discovered various friends on the train and went from carriage to carriage paying calls, while, having provided ourselves with books and writing paper, we were comfortably installed in the restaurant car. We knew from experience that in such barren country one soon gets tired of looking out of the window.

Presently Aramayo came hurrying up to us.

"Look at the vicunas."

"Where?"

"There. In the middle of those llamas. Can't you see three animals paler than the others?"

Jean-Luc, bored with the prospect of another twenty-four hours in the train, was unable to muster much interest, but I drew Aramayo out, getting him to talk about llamas, of which, though we had seen plenty, we still knew little.

"It belongs to the camel family," he said. "It can exist on very little food. It refuses to travel by night. What more can I tell you?"

"What does it eat?"

"Pretty well anything it can find, but chiefly short grass at sundown?"

"Why at sundown?"

"It doesn't get a chance before. The Indians keep driving it on. But though it is a docile animal all day, it digs its toes in in the evening. It sits down and the Indians take its pack off, knowing very well it's useless to try to drive it further. Then it's allowed to wander off on its own, grazing; and in the morning they've only to whistle and it comes back to resume its load."

"Most of the ones we've seen were in pack trains."

"They generally are. They rarely carry more than seventy-five or eighty pounds. So, for bulk transport, such as salt or tin ore, it's more economical for the Indians to pool their llamas in one pack train which sometimes musters as many as two hundred head."

"Where do these llama foetuses come from which we see being sold everywhere?"

It was at that moment that a Jesuit who had overheard our conversation came over to us and, in impeccable French, asked if he might join us.

"And where did you learn to speak French like that?" I asked when he had sat down.

"At Lyons. I did my studies there. But I'm afraid I'm getting very rusty."

"It doesn't sound rusty to me."

A flicker of pride flashed in his keen, intelligent eyes.

"But I'm afraid I've interrupted you," he said. "You were talking of llama foetuses. It's an interesting subject. I know something of Indian customs as I've lived in Bolivia for many years."

But it was Aramayo who explained that the Indians induced abortion in the female llamas by giving them a mush of boiled herbs to eat. It acts immediately—in a few hours; though of course some of the foetuses are the result of a natural miscarriage.

"You may not know that the llama plays a very big part in necromancy. For instance, I've often worked in the mines, and whenever a new seam or a new shaft was opened up the Indians always made me buy a llama to sacrifice at the entrance."

"Isn't it said sometimes that syphilis originated from relations the Indians had with these animals?"

"I don't know much about that, but the llamas are certainly credited here with being carriers of the disease."

"I thought the crusaders brought it back from somewhere," I said.

"I'm afraid that's much nearer the truth," said the Jesuit with a rueful smile.

"How is it that the llama has been domesticated, while its cousins, the vicuna and the alpaca, have remained wild?"

"All I can tell you," answered the priest, "is that it was already like that in the days of the Incas. When the conquistadors arrived they found an organized economy in the country which they tried not to destroy, however much they might pillage and kill. The Inquisition did of course try to extirpate the ancient religious beliefs, in which the llama had an important place, but it didn't succeed in cleansing the Indian mind of all its superstitions."

Environs of La Paz

Chamas Indians

"We have noticed ourselves," said Jean-Luc, "that not only have social customs been refractory to efforts at reform, but that the Indians are still far from being orthodox Catholics. In fact, if you don't mind my saying so, I should say they were still a long way off being Christians of any sort."

"You can't teach me much on that score!" said the Jesuit. "For my part, my work is among students. The important thing, I'm sure, is to create an élite."

He paused, then went on:

"As for the others, we have admittedly had our—our setbacks. I'm not surprised if you've noticed it."

We went on talking in this way all the afternoon. Our new acquaintance felt very keenly on this subject. He had looked deep into Bolivian manners and customs, and we admired the frankness with which he spoke of the problems facing the Church.

My mind reverted to the troop of llamas I had seen near Copacabana, the drivers crying "*Haya, haya,*" as they flourished their long llama-wool cords over the heads of the animals without ever touching them.

"From what we've seen, the Indians never seem to beat their llamas," I remarked.

"It would serve no purpose if they did," answered Aramayo. "They'd get nothing more out of the creatures. The llama's docile enough, but has his limits. If you hit him, he'd simply stop dead in his tracks, and no amount of blows would make him budge another inch."

The priest added:

"You've a saying in France that man domesticated the dog, but the cat domesticated man. One might similarly say that the llama domesticated the Indian, who, incidentally, is well aware of the fact. Before the conquest life on these high plateaux would have been impossible without these beasts of burden."

"If only for providing fuel," I put in, thinking of the llama dung at Jesus de Machaca.

"It's a pity it's not the mating season," said Aramayo. "They've a special *fiesta* for that. It's called *llama-tinku* and takes place in March. Hundreds of llamas are got together for it, and as there are many more males than females the Indians have to be very careful, or twenty males might make for one female, who'd be completely suffocated in the crush."

He also told us that, in coupling, man's intervention was necessary.

"Do you know why?" asked the Jesuit. "If you'll excuse my giving

G

a lecture on anatomy, I can tell you. The sexual organs of both sexes are defective, particularly the male. The penis is curved downwards and unable to reach the vulva, which is in any case too narrow and tightly closed. So men have to come to the rescue, as they do in Europe in the case of some animals."

"Such as the horse," I added.

Whatever the subject, the priest never dried up. Whether it was history, literature, or science, he was a mine of information, and thanks to him the journey we had dreaded turned out to be most agreeable.

Next morning, when we gathered again in the restaurant car, we were surrounded by mountains. The line itself was at this point over 15,000 feet up. We had come through the Condor Pass and were rolling down towards Potosi (13,500).

"We shall soon see the Cerro," said the priest. "It's a famous mine, the richest tin mine in the world. You must visit it. I should like to myself, but the Indians won't allow priests down it—neither priests nor women."

"Why not?"

"They say it would bring bad luck. I could of course go down by putting on civilian clothes. But, if they found me out, the miners would walk out at once and I don't want to be the cause of a row. . . . Look: there's the peak of the Cerro now."

A rust-coloured mountain came into view as the train swept in a wide circle along the valley.

"You'd better get ready. We shall soon be at the station."

When we said good-bye, he told us where we could find him, and pressed us to look him up if there was anything he could do for us. In any case, we were almost bound to meet in a small place like Potosi.

It was bitterly cold there. Dropping our things at the hotel, we went straight off to call on the authorities. It wasn't merely a matter of courtesy: we wanted the use of a car to get round the country districts and we certainly intended making a trip to the Cerro Rico mines.

We encountered no difficulties, and in going the round of the authorities we had our first glimpse of the town. The sun was soon up, banishing the morning chill.

The square in the centre of the town had a formal garden of lawns and clipped hedges, round which were the Prefecture, the Cathedral, and the Theatre. The architecture was less colonial than elsewhere. Going down a narrow street which led to the bishop's palace, we noticed a heavily studded folding door. It opened, and driven by curiosity we went through. Without knowing it, we were in the famous Casa de Moneda.

"Here," I remarked, "one could easily imagine oneself in an old Castilian town, Avila or Segovia." The Spaniards hadn't yet had time to invent a new style, and were content to go on building as they had at home.

Because of the altitude, we dawdled; even so we were soon out of breath, and were glad of an opportunity to sit down in the square and have our shoes cleaned by an Indian boy, who whistled as he polished with a strip of velveteen.

It was in this square that we saw the first Quechuas. These Indians differ little physically from the Aymaras, but their costume is by no means the same. The *ponchos* were much shorter and less voluminous than those we had seen at Jesus de Machaca and La Paz. The wool was coarser and the patterns gaudier. The dominant colour was red, splashed with vertical stripes of yellow, white and black. All the Quechuas went barefoot. Their calves were very dark brown but it was impossible to say whether this colour was natural or merely the result of accumulated dirt. Their cream-coloured breeches stopped just below the knee.

"How do they get them off?" asked Jean-Luc. "They look so tight at the bottom, I don't see how they could."

"They can't. They're sewn on," Aramayo answered. "They're never removed till they're falling to pieces."

The breeches were belted at the top by a woollen cord. There were no fly-buttons, the front closed by two overlapping flaps. Their round hats were rather like priests', brown or black, embroidered with patterns in white representing the sun.

At one corner of the square, we passed a compact group of these people sitting on the ground, basking in the sun. We were appalled by the smell.

"Some of your compatriots don't smell any too good," we said to Aramayo. "But then it must be rather difficult to wash when you can't take your pants off!"

Aramayo laughed.

"They never do."

. . . . . .

After lunch a Ministry of Education car came to fetch us. We were going to a valley which had enjoyed great prosperity in the days of the Incas because of its thermal springs.

On the outskirts of the town we noticed a series of dams which banked up a mass of grey, metallic mud.

"When the Spaniards discovered the Cerro, which the Incas had hardly exploited at all, they weren't after tin but silver," Aramayo explained. "The extraction of the metal was done in a very primitive way, llama dung being used as fuel. The residue was dumped here. What you see is the accumulation of centuries. It contains a high proportion of tin, which might well be extracted. Also a certain amount of silver, but to separate that would be a thankless task."

Our car entered a narrow valley at the bottom of which a mountain torrent roared. Sometimes the road crossed it on small but massively constructed bridges which the chauffeur told us dated from the Incas.

There were many caves in the slopes of the valley and in every cave a cross.

Leaving the main road, we began to climb a winding lane which led, according to a signpost, to the Laguna de Tarapaya, which was one of our objectives. The driver stopped at a stone fountain, also of Inca date, but the spring had either dried up or become blocked, for no water flowed from it now.

The stonework was excellent. Niches cut into the sides showed that as usual the Incas had endowed their work with a religious significance.

The *laguna* was a small natural lake, cut into the side of which was a swimming bath. With a touch of irony we said:

"Naturally the Incas built that too."

"Certainly. But I'm not surprised if you don't believe it. You're not the first. Those stones look as if they had been cut yesterday. And not only was it built by the Incas, but it was built for their own personal use, for them and their families. . . . You can bathe in it if you like, but take care. Plenty of people have been drowned because they swam out into the lake. It's very hot. Indeed it sometimes boils in the middle. Look!"

It was just as he said. We looked, and in the middle of the steaming water we could see a whirlpool of bursting bubbles.

"What's that rope for that runs across the lake?"

"It's for bathers to catch hold of if they do get caught in the whirlpool. You know, there's still a lot of mystery about this lake. No one knows how deep it is, or the reason for that swirling movement, though scientists have been here to study it. For centuries it's been supposed to cure skin diseases and liver troubles. There's another lake in the Chaqui region which does the same."

Indians waiting to cross the Estrecho

Crossing the Estrecho

"I've no skin diseases or liver troubles," said Jean-Luc, "but I think I'd like a dip."

"Not me," I said.

"It's quite safe," said Aramayo, "provided you keep to the swimming bath."

"I dare say, but I'd be afraid of catching cold coming out of that bath into this keen air."

"Perhaps you're wise after all," said Jean-Luc, and we left without anyone having bathed.

Back in the valley we drove for a while alongside the mountain stream. Presently we came to another thermal spring which had been piped, the water being taken across the river to a swimming bath in the garden of a house which had been turned into a restaurant.

We stopped there. We were now a good deal lower than at Potosi, and were glad to sit for a moment basking in the hot sun. We were soon off again, however, as our guide wanted to show us some Inca ruins. Once more we climbed, while the torrent dived into a deep narrow ravine.

We stopped again.

"There!" said the driver.

At first we could see nothing, but he went on pointing, and after a while we were able to make out, on a sort of cylindrical platform in the middle of the gorge, some rectangular structures standing amongst a scanty vegetation.

"Houses?" we asked.

"Perhaps. But a lot of people say they're tombs."

"Hasn't anybody been up to see?"

"No. It's quite inaccessible."

At first sight it certainly seemed so. The rock looked absolutely sheer. As we looked, however, we began to see a lot of small fractures in it which we felt sure would give adequate foothold to a skilled mountaineer.

The more we studied it, the more convinced we became that it could have been nothing less than a fortress. Dominating the valley, it must have served to protect the southern flank of the Inca Empire from invasion from the Argentine.

"Are there any other signs of human life about here?" we asked.

"Only arrow heads. There are plenty of them to be found on the banks of the river."

"There you are! They're houses all right, as the chauffeur says—but for soldiers."

Night was falling when we passed once again the metallic grey mud in the approaches to Potosi. The summit of the Cerro stood up in the last glow of evening daylight.

There were lots of people in the streets of the town.

"Is it always like that?" we asked Aramayo.

"No. It's something special. News of the recent proclamation on Land Reform has just filtered through to this out-of-the-way spot and the Indians are gathering to celebrate it. This is what we call a *concentracion*."

A group in *ponchos* marched by to the music of the *kéna*. I followed them a little way, listening to the haunting, if monotonous, sound of this Indian flute. The men didn't march like soldiers, yet there was something warlike about their gait. They moved as in a martial ballet, lifted up by hope for a social transformation they didn't really understand.

At a word of command they stopped. One of them, catching sight of me, asked:

"Who are you?"

"A foreigner. But I'm with you. I come from the country of liberty."

It crossed my mind that foreigner, to these men, was not far short of meaning enemy. But the man merely asked:

"What's it called, your country?"

"*Francia.*"

Which probably meant nothing to him. What would Bolivia mean to a Burgundian peasant? The man smiled.

"Good!" he said. "I'm afraid you can't come where we're going. It might be dangerous. Thanks, all the same."

A smile from an Indian was not to be despised; thanks was something to be treasured.

.   .   .   .   .

The following morning we went back to the Casa de la Moneda. The stories of the conquest and of Bolivia are written on its walls. The Spaniards built it to coin money for the new territories which Pizarro had won for them. Of its former splendour little remains, though it is now being restored from plans found in the colonial archives at Seville, under the direction of its curator, Señor Alba. The work is being pressed forward and has advanced sufficiently to permit the opening of an interesting museum. But the most arresting part for us was that which contains the enormous wheels, two storeys high, which formed part of the machinery for stamping the money. On the lower floor the Indians of old laboured to turn the wheels, while on the one above (level with the hubs) the Spanish workmen handled the precious metal.

Today the Casa de la Moneda sleeps the sleep of museums.

The afternoon was given up to the Cerro mines. A car belonging to the mining authorities picked us up in front of the Prefecture and drove us off through narrow winding streets of adobe houses before heading for the mountains. On most of the houses I noticed a dark red semicircle with daubs of the same colour round it. I asked what it meant.

"That's llama's blood. The sorcerers paint that sign on to protect the house. It represents the course of the sun in the heavens," answered an employee of the mines who accompanied us.

We came to the foot of a mountain, every square yard of which showed evidence of the hand of man, having been worked over and over in the course of ages. In the little streams men were still washing out old silver-bearing veins. The whole scene was one of indescribable chaos, a jumble of red rocks and grey rocks tumbling over each other in all directions. Here and there were dark holes through which miners went in and out.

A sky of purest blue, an air of the purest cold, a landscape of desolation—that's the Cerro de Potosi.

We stopped in front of a small building at a place where several narrow-gauge railway lines converged. There we found a delegate of the Bolivian Mining Corporation, who gave us some information. Then we questioned one of the engineers.

"Since when have the mines been nationalized?"

"Since November 1952. The revolution in April of that year was chiefly backed by the miners, whose aim was to wrench the mines from the hands of the three great proprietors."

"Do they all belong to the state now?"

"Not all. This one does. Some of them, like the San Jose de Oruro, were put in the hands of a workers' co-operative."

"How many men have you got working in the Cerro?"

A vague answer. Several thousand certainly. Prolonged absentee-ism would in any case make an accurate figure difficult to obtain.

Miners often stop work indefinitely when they have a little money put by, returning to the mine only when the fund is exhausted. There are others who, at harvest time, go off for a couple of months with their wives, children, and llamas, to bring home a few bushels of potatoes. Others stay away on account of sickness, conditions being most unhygienic. Pulmonary diseases are common, and the arsenical gases, abundant in these mines, often lead to fatal illnesses. Few miners live beyond the age of forty.

A man came in. Another engineer, dressed in typical mining clothes, with a helmet. A miner followed, carrying three similar suits for us.

Aramayo, who had had a lot of mining experience, showed us how to put them on and adjust the battery for the little lamp in the helmet. Thus kitted up, we were taken into a long level tunnel whose walls glistened with damp.

"How high are we here?" asked Jean-Luc.

"Over thirteen thousand feet."

A short distance from the entrance we saw a niche cut in the rock wall, in which was a horned statue made of dried mud, feebly lit by a few candles; the light also revealed a variety of objects, food, and cigarettes.

"What's all that stuff for?"

"To propitiate the demons that dwell in the mines," answered our guide. "The miners are constantly seeing them, and when they don't see them they hear them. The only thing they can do about it is to try to keep them happy. So they bring cigarettes, which the bad spirits smoke with the help of the draught of air. Also food and coca leaves."

We walked miles to the sound of trickling water and rumbling ore trucks which echoed from the rock face, before we finally reached the lifts.

Then we went down—hundreds of feet, thousands of feet—the temperature rising all the time. At the bottom it was almost unbearable, 102 degrees Fahrenheit. It was an effort to walk, an effort to breathe. What with sweat and dripping water, we were soaked through.

At the end of a gallery was a faint light. Coming to it, we found half a dozen miners, working with picks and drills, sounding for a vein. They wore nothing but pants, which clung limply to their thighs as if they had just stepped out of a bath. And they worked like that in putrid air for eleven hours at a stretch!

We spoke little, feeling that at any minute we might sink to the ground suffocated. Nevertheless one of us asked:

"What's that funny smell?"

"A mixture of noxious gases."

"Don't they do anything to ventilate the galleries?"

"Only this."

We were shown a miserable little pipe through which foetid air was blowing.

"How do these fellows stand it?"

"They chew coca. That keeps them going. But we're hoping to transform the whole system of ventilation. This is a legacy from the bad old days."

We went back to the lift, by no means sorry to leave that inferno of heat, damp, and dust.

A few galleries higher, while we were changing lifts, Jean-Luc suddenly turned pale and had to lie down for a while.

What struck us most was the emptiness of the mine. We hardly saw anybody. The engineer showing us round explained that the workers, whether mining or prospecting, were scattered about in small groups of not more than five or six.

"Don't you think the Indians are quite different down here?" I asked Jean-Luc. "They don't seem like Indians at all."

"No. You have to think of that shrine to the demons to remember what they are. Here in the mine they're simply miners."

At the top we walked a short distance, then got onto the little electric engine that dragged the ore trucks. We had to take care, as the rock was sometimes only a few inches above our heads, to say nothing of the live wire which didn't look any too safe.

At the entrance to the mine we were greeted by an icy night wind. And to think that the miners had to face that every day, stepping straight out of a furnace into eighteen degrees of frost—a sudden drop of 108 degrees!

Once again we asked:

"How do they stand it?"

"They don't. Not really. Most of them die young—about forty—of bronchial pneumonia or pleurisy."

We realized this was taken very much to heart by the people who were trying to bring into line with modern notions of human welfare an industry which hitherto had had one aim—to 'make the *poncho* sweat'.

IX

The Quechuas at Home

THERE had been trouble with the Quechua Indians, and nobody was at all inclined to provide a car when we said we wanted to visit them, to compare their customs with those of the Aymaras.

We knocked at several doors in vain. At last, however, a school inspector agreed to lend us one.

"But not for more than two days," he said, "and then only if you promise to come back to Potosi for the night."

Though we didn't like that condition we had no choice but to accept. We regretted not having made greater efforts at La Paz to keep our old jeep and the Macho. Efforts at persuasion were unavailing: the inspector remained adamant.

"You never know," he said. "If there was a rising during the night, the Indians might well wreck the car."

There was quite a lot of talk about Indian risings. Most of it was without foundation, yet the stories were circulating more and more freely.

When we drove off next morning, we headed for the Cerro, then swerved to the left and climbed several miles to a pass. All round us, the mountains were a beautiful tawny colour. Scared by the sound of the motor, a flock of birds flew up.

"They live in the ground," said Aramayo. "They dig holes for themselves, to get out of the wind. They're easy to catch in the early morning."

From the pass, the road ran down a long, narrow valley. The landscape changed. The mountains turned beige. Here and there were llamas grazing on the short grass. The valley grew still narrower, till we were in an arid gorge. A few tufts of grass grew in the dust by the roadside, otherwise all was jagged rock, towering up steep on either hand.

At the bottom roared a blue mountain torrent. Here and there in the rock wall were entrances to a mine, looking like human burrows. Some were so high up that we wondered how the miners reached them. Only by looking very carefully could we make out the narrow paths hacked out of the rock.

Down we went, till we were at an altitude of less than eleven thousand. Then the valley widened. The grass became thicker, but it was still that dried-up beige colour.

Then came the cacti, sticking up several yards high, the branched ones looking like archaic candlesticks.

All at once we had to stop, the road being completely blocked by a large herd of llamas. Jean-Luc pounced on the opportunity to film them. To fill in the time, I teased some, hoping to make them spit, but they treated me with lordly indifference.

"*Haya! Haya!*" cried the Indians.

No amount of coaxing could clear our path. As soon as one llama was driven past the car and the drover turned to deal with another, the first would dash back, going right round the herd to take his place in the rear. Again and again the same thing happened.

"Do you remember what the Jesuit said? It's no earthly use hitting them. The leaders of the herd are scared. As soon as they find out the car's harmless, they'll go by, and all the others will follow."

"You speak of the leaders. Are they like sheep?"

"Exactly. With one difference, however. In the case of sheep there's *a* leader of the herd. With llamas there are several."

The Indians driving them, two men and an old woman, were quite ready to be filmed. They were extraordinarily ragged. You could see the men's thighs through their breeches, great ribbons of which hung down over their calves, and little was left of the solar symbols embroidered on their hats—unless they were hidden under a thick layer of dirt.

"What are those little coloured balls that some of the llamas have on their ears?"

"They tell you who the animal belongs to. As I've already told you, the Indians often pool their llamas for the dispatch of goods in bulk. Sometimes there are even more than these."

"And there are a good two hundred here," added Jean-Luc.

As Aramayo had predicted, some of the llamas began to think better of the car and walked quietly past, followed by the others. The old woman had disappeared down into the valley to round up some of the more frightened animals, who had made off altogether. When she reappeared she was climbing up the slope with the same agility she had shown in the reverse direction. All along, the Indians had taken the situation very calmly. They showed no resentment against us for having caused such a disturbance.

"Standing still with its head raised," said Jean-Luc, "the llama looks very like a camel, but when it jumps from rock to rock it reminds one more of a goat."

We agreed.

As we drove on, the landscape changed once again. Used as we were to the monotony of the Altiplano and Lake Titicaca, these sudden shifts of scene took us by surprise. The cacti gave way to eucalyptus trees; the horizon broadened; a few more hairpin bends and we were out on a vast plain. In the distance was the belfry of a village church.

"What's the name of that village?"

"Belen."

The chauffeur, much less communicative than the Macho had been, volunteered no further information. We went through a small eucalyptus wood whose leaves fluttered in the least breath of wind. Through the open windows of the car came puffs of sultry air, heavy with the scent of the trees.

Just outside Belen was a fine house in colonial style standing alone surrounded by an exceptionally high adobe wall, which gave it almost the air of a fortress. At the time when Potosi was pouring its silver into the coffers of Spain, some *hidalgo* had perhaps chosen this spot to hide away his spoils of conquest.

The houses on the outskirts of the village were scattered, but they huddled closer and closer together as we advanced, till in the rather wide main street they formed two solid ranks. Suddenly an archway across the street barred our passage: an old town gate, built to the measure of the wagons of former days, so narrow that our car could only just squeeze through; on the other side, a square with a school.

We had a look at the school, an adobe building, like all the others. Like the furniture too. The little Indians sat on adobe benches at adobe desks. The schoolmistress was quite flustered when Aramayo introduced us as foreign professors. When she recovered her composure she made the children sing us a song. As they sang, their bodies swayed from side to side to mark the rhythm.

Further on was another square, much bigger than the first. A wall ran right across one side. Behind it was the church. Its size astonished us. It seemed to us out of all proportion to the population of the village.

"In colonial times," Aramayo explained, "there were rich Spanish settlers in these parts, rich enough to secure a place in heaven by

Indian girl

Dancers at Copacabana

building one of these huge churches. Let's go and get the key. There's another school here, run by the church, and the teacher keeps the key."

She unlocked the door for us, but it was so heavy (and warped into the bargain) that we had to join forces to push it open. The interior presented a lamentable appearance. The wooden altars were worm-eaten and dilapidated, the statues were all over the place, their limbs scattered on the floor. It had certainly been rich in its day. Two pictures by a disciple of El Greco were gradually disintegrating.

"Why do they leave them here?" we asked. "They should be taken to the Casa de Moneda where they could be looked after."

"The curator wanted to," said the schoolmistress, "but the priest wouldn't give his consent."

"Is there a priest here?"

"Yes. But he doesn't live in the village, and he doesn't come here often. Practically never."

"Do you know how old the church is?"

"At least eight hundred years."

We were too polite to contradict her!

We couldn't stop long, as our visit to the Quechuas was a race against time. We had still a little way to go across the wide plain, which, contrasted with the Altiplano, could better be described as rolling country. We were now not much over 8,000 feet up and the climate was quite different.

Asked the name of the region, Aramayo answered:

"We've just left the Puna behind us. But you could say we're still there, as the town we're making for is called Puna, too. As you know, the mountain-sickness, called *sorache* at La Paz, is called *puna* here. As a matter of fact, it is often claimed that there are really two distinct illnesses, not one, that of the Potosi region differing on account of its soil being so rich in metals. It seems they have an effect on the human organism."

"I hadn't thought of it before," I said, "but Keyserling in his book on South America only speaks of *puna*. What do you think, Jean-Luc? Do you feel the altitude here in the same way as at La Paz?"

"To tell the truth, apart from that sudden attack in the mine, I've felt nothing at all in this region, whereas I never felt well at La Paz. But tell me, Aramayo, do any Bolivians suffer from mountain-sickness? Or rather from *puna* or *sorache*, for what we call mountain-sickness in Europe is really quite different."

"Yes. But those who are upset at La Paz aren't in the least at Potosi and vice-versa. That's why we have two different words."

"Certainly Jean-Luc is quite right in distinguishing our mountain-sicknesses from either of these two. One day, when I was doing quite a modest climb with a girl, I got a violent headache at just over 8,000 feet. It was as though my head was in a vice. It passed off as quickly as it had come. But I got it again in the Chamonix area each time I went to that height. As for the girl, she felt nothing at all till we were further up. Then, at about 10,000 feet, she fell to the ground, white as a sheet, retching, and mumbling incomprehensibly. When we came down a bit she recovered at once. That's very different from anything you experienced at La Paz, isn't it?"

"Yes," said Jean-Luc. "The whole of the right side of my body felt paralysed."

"It wasn't. You moved all right."

"I know. But that's what I felt like—a sort of numbness, mixed with shivers, and pins and needles."

At that moment our driver emerged from his silence to point out a village we were passing which stood back from the road.

"There was a rising there. There are a lot of *fincas* round here. The Indians burnt the owners' houses. They were very angry. They even burnt the church."

"Can we go and see?"

We always liked to verify such stories when possible.

"You can go on foot if you like. I'm responsible for the car."

That would have taken too long. Soon after, when the road forked, we turned right, and, a little further on, came to a large building, very white and undoubtedly of recent construction. Across it was written Nucleo Escolar, Alcatuyo.

"There's no one there," said the chauffeur simply.

At the same moment we saw a number of low houses on our left, scattered over a wide area. They were Indian dwellings.

Mistrustful of the chauffeur's capacity as guide, Jean-Luc said:

"Wouldn't it be as well to stop to see if those houses constitute a community?"

The chauffeur's answer was blunt:

"It's not. Besides, we've got to get to Puna. There you'll find all the *ayllus* you want."

We had all along been speaking of communities, having got into the habit among the Aymaras. But we remembered that *ayllu* was the word used in Quechua.

The first houses of Puna were already in sight. The town was divided into two distinct parts, one in the plain, the other on a low hill. The trees, scattered about everywhere, seemed strange after the nakedness of the Altiplano.

A central square, much like that of Potosi, though humbler. The car drew up at a one-storey building bearing the arms of Bolivia. On a sky-blue oval plaque, we could read that this was the Sub-Prefecture of Puna in the province of Linares.

Getting out of the car, we noticed that the scent of eucalyptus trees had followed us here. The air was full of it. The heat was quite different here from what we had found in Potosi; there, even in the midday sun, the air never lost its keenness.

We sent the chauffeur in to announce our arrival. He returned promptly to say that the Sub-Prefect would be pleased to see us. We went in and crossed an interior courtyard with an ill-kept garden.

A middle-aged man received us in a room which had the proportions of an over-wide corridor. A sofa and some easy chairs in worn-out imitation leather gave the impression of a lawyer's waiting-room in one of Balzac's novels. The dinginess of it all was enhanced by contrast with the brutal glare outside.

He found it difficult to understand our interest in the Indians. He confused ethnology and geology, and then geology and geography. When we mentioned sociology, he thought we were talking of socialism. We could see he was taken aback and even rather annoyed that such dangerous people should be recommended to him by the Minister of Education. To dodge us he said that it was the headmaster of the school whom we should see.

He sent someone off to fetch the man in question, who promptly appeared. He was just the opposite, understanding at once what we wanted, and anxious to give what help he could, though he warned us he hadn't been long in the district. We soon got down to brass tacks.

"Do the Indians live in communities here?"

"Yes, though they're called *ayllus* here."

"How many are there in Puna?"

"Six."

"Can you tell us their names, and what the names mean, if they have a meaning?"

He reeled them off at once.

"Karoma, which means The Great Ayllu; Suraga; Marca Suraga (*marca* means village); Toaka; Kassa, meaning cold; Aisoko."

"A most important thing we want to know is whether the customs are the same throughout the whole of this region. Are they the same here as at Chaqui, for instance?"

"Yes, and at Alcatuyo too, with just this difference that it's probably at Alcatuyo that they are the best preserved."

"Alcatuyo? But we've just passed it. Our driver said it wasn't a community at all. Perhaps we could go there tomorrow."

"Do. And I'll warn the schoolmaster you're coming, and tell him to gather together the *curacas* and any others likely to provide useful information. Alcatuyo is not only an *ayllu*, but it's an independent one, which is rare."

"You spoke of *curacas* . . ."

"Yes. They're the chiefs. Like the *ilacatas* in the Aymara districts. If you'd like to see one, I can produce a *curaca* at once. Come out into the courtyard; you can interview him there. I'll send for him."

We took our leave of the Sub-Prefect, who had been blatantly dozing during our conversation. By the time we had got into the courtyard there was the *curaca* of Karoma, whom the schoolmaster introduced. We were greeted with the faintest of smiles. The *curaca* wore a *poncho* decidedly smaller than those of the Aymaras, so short that we could see the top of his trousers. His clothes were in fact the same as those we had seen worn in the main square of Potosi. His insignia differed little from those carried by the *ilacatas*—a cross on his chest and a baton inlaid with silver.

"What do you call your baton here?"

He spoke a little Spanish.

"*Barra.*"

"Why is it the sign of a chief?"

"Manco Capac had one too, but his was gold."

We were astonished at this answer. What should he know of the great Emperor?

"Who was Manco Capac?" asked Jean-Luc, feigning ignorance.

"The Inca."

"Who told you?"

"My grandfather's father."

"And who told him?"

"His grandfather. He said so."

Quetchua Indian

Negroes of the Yungas

Evidently he hadn't learnt the name in school or from the lips of any white man. This was a real case of ancestral lore.

His smile was a little less faint now. He was obviously only too ready to answer any questions we might ask. Unlike Jesus de Machaca, here we did not have to spend several days winning the natives' confidence. So we got straight down to the organization of communities, leaving other customs until tomorrow at Alcatuyo, where, according to the schoolmaster, they were better preserved.

"Who elected you, *Curaca*?"

"All the men of the *ayllu* between nineteen and sixty."

"For how long?"

"One year."

The same as at Jesus de Machaca, only the procedure was different. There the *ilacatas* were elected, not by a popular vote, but by co-optation.

"If a *curaca* dies, can his wife take his place?"

"No. There has to be another election."

"Do you run the *ayllu* single-handed, or have you got assistants?"

"Assistants, yes. A *cacique*, three *principals*, three district *alcades*, and three *alcades*."

"Are they elected in the same way as you are?"

"Yes. Just the same."

As with an *ilacata* at Jesus de Machaca, a *curaca* must have filled all the other posts in the *ayllu* before becoming the supreme chief.

"Do you work during your period of office, *Curaca*?"

"Yes. But only for myself."

"How can one distinguish a *cacique*?"

"Two silver stripes on his *poncho*."

Our informant was getting tired. He had increasing difficulty with his Spanish, and his smile grew rarer. Lunch was not yet ready but we invited the schoolmaster and the Sub-Prefect to have a *pisco* with us. We ordered a drink for the *curaca* and told him to wait for us, promising to drive him back to his *ayllu*.

The Sub-Prefect came out of his coma and accompanied us to a little shop in a corner of the square.

"What *pisco*!" we exclaimed. "We've never had any like it."

Aramayo, who was a connoisseur, agreed.

"It's said to be the best in all Bolivia," said the schoolmaster.

"Is it local? Is it warm enough here for vines?"

H

"We get any amount of sun here and vines do excellently, and so do many other fruits."

The Sub-Prefect nodded contentedly.

.   .   .   .   .

After lunch we took the *curaca* of Karoma back to his *ayllu*, which was not far from Puna. As we went, we realized how much this more temperate region had in common with Jesus de Machaca. The houses, though smaller, were substantially the same; so, in general, was the farming, though certain crops could ripen here which were unknown on the Altiplano: maize, wheat, beans, and fruit. The same animals were bred with the addition of donkeys and guinea-pigs, which incidentally came originally from this country.

"If Europeans knew how much had come to them from South America, they'd wonder what their ancestors had to eat."

"And if they were to consider how little is indigenous to Europe," answered Jean-Luc, "they'd be astonished at what prehistoric man had to eat."

We were interested to know what products had to be brought from elsewhere.

"What do you buy that you can't produce yourself?"

"Sugar . . . rice . . . spirits . . . salt . . ."

The *curaca* pondered for a moment, then added:

"Bread for the *fiestas*, and flour."

"What about coca? Do you grow it?"

"Oh no. I buy that too."

An old woman was sitting outside her front door grinding a grey powder between two round stones.

"Who is she?"

"My mother."

We went up to her and greeted her, but she knew no Spanish and could only smile back.

"What's she doing?"

"Making coca quids."

She ground it to a fine powder with chalk and ash. This she put in an old tin and mixed with water to a paste, which was rubbed through a strainer with the tip of a stone. The strainer was simply a tin the bottom of which was riddled with holes. What came through she worked, rather like pastry, folding the paste over and rolling it out with the round stones. When thick enough, she rolled it out for the last time and cut it into small rectangles, using for this a spoon (kept under her shawl) whose handle had been whetted to a point as sharp as a needle.

The rectangles were then left to dry. They were the quids. When dry they would go into one of those little bags which the Indians carry about with them.

"Who owns the land here, *Curaca*?" we asked.

"Everybody has his own land. When he dies it is divided equally among all his children."

We thought of the custom we had been told about at Jesus de Machaca—the *aynoka*—and wondered whether anything similar existed here.

"Is any part of the land worked by the whole community in common?"

"Yes," answered the *curaca*. "We call it *faena*. All work together on one man's land. But it has to be virgin soil."

"Who gathers in the harvest?"

"The man who owns the land."

That was interesting. At Jesus de Machaca, the *aynoka* crops were divided among everybody.

"Does the owner of the land give anything in exchange?"

"Yes, he gives a *fiesta*. For everybody."

Another aspect of the *fiesta*, which has so many—political, economic, social, and religious.

Politically it gathers together all the members of a community and makes them conscious of their solidarity.

Economically it pools their narrow surplus of wealth—spirits, coca, food, glittering costumes.

Socially it makes them aware of the role which each has to play in the community and of the benefits which accrue from common effort.

But above all the *fiesta* is of religious significance. After long months of toil and privation, the banked-up spiritual forces break out. Hostilities disappear, restraint is dropped, and all are swept along together in an outburst of delirious joy.

Throughout the stark and monotonous year the *fiesta* shines as a beacon of hope, without which life would be unendurable. One finds the same thing in the carnivals of Brazil and of the West Indies, or, looking back, in those of Rome and Venice.

Our chauffeur was beginning to show signs of impatience.

"We've got to get back to Potosi before the barriers are closed. And we've still got Chaqui to do."

"What barriers?"

"The customs. They close the barriers every night to prevent metal smuggling."

So we said good-bye to the *curaca* and headed for Chaqui, where we arrived an hour later. We had no time to lose. A few Indians were sauntering about the main square. The authorities, warned by telegram of our visit, had organized a reception. At the school, the children sang the Bolivian national anthem, then marched round the playground. We went the round of the classrooms where the teachers showed us their pupils' work, including some admirable drawings, particularly those done by the little ones.

When we got back to the square, the Sub-Prefect was waiting to take us to the Town Hall, where bottles of beer were ready. Though touched by this solicitude, we longed to get on with our real work. Time was slipping by and we were afraid of being hurried off by our chauffeur.

"How many *ayllus* are there at Chaqui?" I asked.

The Sub-Prefect answered that the best thing was to go and ask the Indians on the Square.

We found three there, who gazed at us with mild curiosity. All had two silver stripes on their *ponchos*; in other words they were *caciques*.

"Tell us the names of the *ayllus*, will you?"

All three began speaking at once and it wasn't easy to get the names disentangled, but we finally drew up a list of them.

The *caciques*, all young men, confirmed what the *curaca* had told us at Puna. Unfortunately, the chauffeur was by now anxious to be off. To prolong our conversation, however, we offered a lift to one of the *caciques* whose home was some distance off along the road we had to take. He, of course, was delighted. On our way we plied him with questions, the chauffeur acting as interpreter.

Remembering what Warachi had said about the dead, we brought the conversation round to that subject.

"Do the dead often come back?"

"Yes. We see them sometimes, and they look just the same as they did before. They're quite harmless and no one's afraid of them. Only babies that die unbaptized—they're dangerous. They change into gnomes and frighten children. One always meets them in the same places. But not so often nowadays."

"Are there any other spirits?"

"Only devils. They go about at night and if you meet one you go mad."

The *cacique* told us when to turn, and at the end of a little lane we came to the community of Pakaja. A small square, a little chapel. A few of the houses had grey stone foundations. Here and there a tree, reminding us once again that we were far from the Altiplano. The *curaca* of the *ayllu* came to meet us, carrying his silver-studded baton, and surrounded by his assistants.

We should have loved to stop, but the chauffeur was firm. We must get back to Potosi. We had just time to hand round some cigarettes, and we were off.

We drove back as fast as the state of the road allowed. The driver, now that he had his way, became quite talkative. Pointing in the direction of Lake Chaqui, he told us its water was known all over Bolivia as being good for liver troubles. It gushes boiling out of the ground and is bottled in a small factory, where they also make a sort of lemonade called *chaqui*.

.   .   .   .   .

We had arranged to start off again at six next morning, and punctually at that time the car drew up in front of our hotel. We took the same road again and reached Alcatuyo at eight. The headmaster was waiting for us, having been told to expect us. He insisted on our meeting all the teachers and inspecting the school buildings.

"I'm beginning to have had enough of schools," whispered Jean-Luc in my ear.

But there was no help for it: the headmaster had made his arrangements and the Indians didn't figure on the programme till the afternoon. The best we could do was to get him to give us an early lunch so that we could get down to our real work as soon as possible.

.   .   .   .   .

When we got up from the luncheon table, the midday sun was beating down at its fiercest, the heat reflected from every wall. Outside, a few Indians awaited us by the side of the road. The eldest had on his face an expression of the utmost reserve, yet without either hardness or cruelty. All were barefoot, and Jean-Luc, intrigued by their nodulous ankles and toes, at once got busy with the camera.

We settled down and took out our notebooks. We wanted to enquire into Indian customs and determine the influence which religion had exerted on them, but first of all we wished to find out the importance of this *ayllu* and what were its relations with others in the neighbourhood.

"How many people live in Alcatuyo?"

"About five thousand."

"So many in a single *ayllu*?"

"Yes."

"You're not linked to any group of *ayllus*?"

"No. We're absolutely independent."

Our interpreter emphasised the word 'absolutely', as the *curaca* had done.

"Is the *ayllu* divided up into parts?"

"Yes. In two parts. But both parts come under me," said the *curaca*.

"Has it always been so?"

"Not always. A long time ago there used to be two *curacas*, one for each part."

We seemed to have two *ayllus* here which had been fused into a single unit. We tried to find out how this had happened, but our informers could throw no light on the problem.

"It's so long ago," was all they could say.

"Are you Catholics?"

"Yes," they answered in chorus.

"Where does the priest live?"

"At Puna. But he's never there. He comes there from time to time just to collect his money. He spends it in the big town. He hasn't been there long. The man before did just the same."

They didn't sound enthusiastic about the chap.

"Are you dissatisfied with your priests?" we asked.

"When the old one was here," came the answer, "a hundred of us paid for masses. A thousand bolivianos (ten shillings) each. Then he called us all together and said one mass for the lot, instead of a hundred. As it happened, he died next day, and we all went in a body and took the money back. We built a school with it."

The *curaca* showed us a printed sheet.

"I went up to the bishop's palace in Potosi and asked how much we ought to be charged for baptisms, marriages, and funerals. I was given this. The prices down here are only a half what the priest had been making us pay."

As we looked at the list, he added:

"From now on, we're not going to have the priest for funerals. We can do it just as well without him."

The readiness with which our questions were answered encouraged us to probe into the various phases of Indian life.

"Tell us about childbirth. How is it managed?"

"The women who are older and have had experience help the mother and wash the baby as soon as it's born."

Recalling the religious and magic significance of the afterbirth at Jesus de Machaca, we asked what was done with it here.

"The women who help take it and wash it till the water's quite clear. Then they bury it in the house with various things. If it's a girl, with a thimble, a needle, and a little pot. If it's a boy, with an exercise book, pencils, a spade, pick, and anvil."

"What? Real ones?"

"Oh no. The big things aren't real, just models made of clay."

Each object had of course its symbolic meaning, designed to influence the future development of the child.

"Do women often have twins here?"

"No. Very rarely. If they're both boys or both girls, that's lucky. If they're a boy and a girl, that's a bad omen."

Weddings, we learnt, went off in much the same way as in the Aymara districts. They were occasions when each tried to win prestige in the eyes of his neighbours, a vast competition in generosity in fact.

The same could be said of wakes and funerals. The more drink or coca distributed, the more esteem accrued. And conversely, the more a family respected itself, the more must it give.

At Alcatuyo, too, people believed in the reappearance of the dead. And here again meticulous care was given to the disposal of the deceased's clothing. Seven days after the death, the clothes were washed in the river. Those which were serviceable were distributed amongst the family, the remainder being burnt. If the latter were burnt without first being washed, the soul of the dead man or woman would have great difficulty in getting into heaven.

"How does one become a sorcerer?" we asked.

"There are three ways. Sometimes a sorcerer passes the power on to his son. Sometimes it's by thunder and lightning."

When the lightning strikes down just beside a man, he's ready to become a sorcerer. He faints and then comes to, or, as the Indians say, he's 'undone' and then 'remade', by which they mean that he has undergone a profound change. After it, he's a sorcerer. Where the lightning has struck, they told us, a white stone will be found in the ground.

"The third way is to get the power from a sorcerer who looks after you when you're ill."

"How do they cure illnesses?"

"They use herbs, lizards, and earth. They find out what's the matter by reading it in coca leaves or cards."

The time slipped by all too quickly. Like a bird of ill omen, our chauffeur was soon hovering about, anxious to be off. We knew by now that it was useless to argue with him.

That evening, after dinner, various officials called on us to say good-bye as we were taking the train back to La Paz that night.

X

The Negroes of the Yungas

WE were only intending to stay a few days at La Paz—just long enough to arrange our journey into Peru. But the many formalities to be gone through and the fact that the trains only ran intermittently combined to delay our departure and give us an opportunity of paying a visit to the Yungas.

Again and again, during our travels in Bolivia, we had been asked: "Do you know the Yungas?"

All we knew was that they were tropical valleys situated at no great distance from the capital, valleys generally regarded by the Bolivians of the Altiplano as a sort of paradise, being only 8,000 feet up and correspondingly warm.

Once again we were lent the jeep which had taken us to Jesus de Machaca, and with it the Macho.

We decided to spend forty-eight hours in this blissful region.

To start with, however, we had to climb across a range of bare mountains of a pale rusty colour. Though the road was a proper mountain one, twisting back and forth, the gradient was steep and the car advanced slowly. A car, just like a human being, suffers from high altitudes—over 10,000 feet it loses half its power.

Suddenly we found ourselves at the top, over 16,000 feet up, on a little flattened hump belonging to a somewhat shapeless mountain. On either side of the ridge numerous valleys ran down, either towards La Paz or the Yungas, but on the side of the latter it was still impossible to see any sign of the tropical paradise we had been promised.

The Macho smiled as he stopped the car near a stone cross on the highest point of the hump. He had often spoken of his fondness for the Yungas.

"Tonight you won't need to bother about blankets or warm clothing," he said. "In the Yungas you can just lie down on the ground anywhere and go to sleep. It's always nice there."

And he added:

"That's why the Negroes settled there."

We started on the downward drive. The road, though not surfaced, was reasonably good though dangerous. The Macho warned us we should be skirting formidable precipices all the way. For this reason it was a one-way road, the morning in one direction, the afternoon in the other.

"I'm stone deaf," I exclaimed presently.

So were Jean-Luc, Aramayo and the Macho.

"There's a customs post a little further on," said Aramayo. "We'd better stop there and have a drink. That's the only way to get rid of this buzzing in one's ears."

"A customs post? What for?"

"Coca."

"I thought there was no restriction on the coca trade," said Jean-Luc.

"There isn't. But the authorities like to keep statistics. Practically all the coca chewed in Bolivia is grown in the Yungas and has to pass along this road."

The mountains rose sharply on either side, but we hadn't yet seen anything of the Macho's precipices. Close to the road ran a little mountain stream gushing over a stony bed.

The gorge became narrower and narrower, and then, after a bend, we came to some buildings—the customs post, a restaurant, some offices, and opposite, almost in the stream, some wooden huts built by Indians or half-caste traders who sold refreshments and various commodities such as stuffs and clothing.

We drew up at the restaurant and ordered a copious breakfast. I then went off in search of cigarettes. On my return, I found Jean-Luc and Aramayo chatting with a couple of priests who were travelling in the other direction.

"But it's not allowed. You can't go that way till the afternoon," we expostulated.

"Admittedly," they answered, "but no one's stopped us yet. And it isn't the first time we've done it."

They were very friendly and told us quite a lot about the Yungas and where we could find hotels.

"You mustn't miss seeing the Negroes there. And the school of agriculture at Chulumani. It's run by Redemptorists. They're doing very interesting work there—carrying out a lot of experiments."

We were intending to make Chulumani our first stop, and we promised to visit the school.

The valley broadened, and the road wound lazily along it. But there were still no palms or banana trees and we were beginning to wonder whether the accounts of this El Dorado were not somewhat exaggerated.

But now at last we found ourselves running along a sloping cliff with, far below us, a rushing torrent, blue and white.

Soon we were at the bottom, with the cliff now towering above us. On the other side was a forest, surprising only in coming upon us so suddenly after the arid flora of the Altiplano and the Andes.

At several places in the cliff water spurted out, falling in a fine spray over the road.

"Just what we want," said the Macho. "I'll stop for a moment to give the car a wash, to get rid of some of this mountain dust."

He sat smiling in the car as the water pattered down on it. There was no doubt about it—the Yungas did him good. Now that we were there nothing could cloud his sunny mood.

Soon the road passed houses standing in gardens planted with trees and full of flowers.

"*Fincas.* Belonging to rich men in La Paz. Nice places to spend a week-end in. The farming's not taken too seriously."

Chulumani. We dropped our bags at the hotel and set off to explore the place, and first of all the school of agriculture situated just above the town. The road wound up to it through real tropical vegetation, ending at a large modern-looking building which impressed us. There had been no cheeseparing in its construction. As we drove up to it, we skirted a garden full of roses and other flowers.

"May we see the Father Superior?" asked Aramayo.

A rather chilly response—the Father Superior was very busy. Still, he received us very politely in his tiny office. His rough, knobbly hands were evidently used to hard work. His nails were black with earth. His clothes, to which he obviously gave very little thought, were covered with spots, presumably from the chemicals in his laboratory. Cold as his manner was, he was unable to conceal the intense pride he took in his school.

After a few minutes' talk he turned us over to one of his pupils, a boy of about eighteen, who, on his side, didn't conceal his unbounded admiration for his master.

"You know," he said, "the Father Superior's a great inventor. We'll go first of all to the poultry house, and I'll show you something he invented years ago."

And with reverential awe he added:

"*El tubo a criar los pollos.*" The tube to create the pullets. In less picturesque terms, an incubator.

The hen-house was certainly very well laid out on modern lines and as clean as a hen-house can possibly be.

"But where's the Father Superior's invention?" I asked.

"We're just coming to it."

Our guide solemnly opened a door.

"There! *El tubo a criar los pullos!* He invented it."

"Did he invent central heating too?"

"Come on, come on," said Aramayo, smothering his laughter. "Don't be unkind. If you must say things like that, say them in French."

Unconscious of any offence, our guide showed us all round the place, finishing up with the flower garden, where he said:

"Here's another of his inventions. He grafts rose on to *escaramujo.*"

We neither of us knew what the word meant. When we asked Aramayo he answered:

"I don't know what you call it in French, but it's the wild rose."

Leaving the atmosphere of hero-worship, we went back to our hotel. We decided to have a lazy evening, and when dinner was over we went straight to bed.

.   .   .   .   .

It was during the next day's drive that we came to the real precipices. Again and again we found ourselves looking straight down into a valley three thousand feet below. The vegetation everywhere was luxuriant, but we were used to it by now and took little notice of it.

"This is Murita we're coming to, a village entirely peopled by Blacks."

"Where did they come from?"

Aramayo told us that long ago some of the Negro slaves of Brazil escaped from their plantations and, working their way up the Amazon and the Madeira, reached the Beni. Even there, they didn't feel that they had put enough distance between them and their former masters, and they only came to a final halt in the Yungas.

We got out of the jeep in front of the church, the door of which was open. We went in. The only remarkable thing we found was the statue of a Negro over the high altar.

"Who is that saint?"

"Saint Benito, the patron saint of the Negroes."

We wondered why St. Benedict should have been chosen as their patron saint. Aramayo was not at a loss for an answer.

"Because he once said, speaking of the Ethiopians: '*Niger sed sapiens*—black but wise.'"

One needn't be surprised. St. Cecilia became the patron saint of musicians on just as slender grounds. On the way to her execution, she sang *in her heart* the praises of the Saviour.

Leaving the church, we looked about for someone to talk to. The Negroes had all adopted the language and costume of the Aymaras. Africans in *ponchos*. They also spoke Spanish.

The women wore the white blouses and short skirts of the Aymaras. It was not without its funny side. These women with frizzy hair, their babies on their arms, still looked so very different from the people of the Altiplano.

They were very approachable and only too ready to be photographed.

"You know, they've got a king," said the Macho.

We promptly questioned a man who had been following us, fascinated by our cameras.

"We did have one," he answered, "but he died four months ago. We haven't yet chosen another. It's a dying custom. But if you like I can take you to see the princess, the last king's daughter."

He came with us to the car and we all got in. As we drove along, the Macho constantly addressed him as *Rubio*. We were somewhat surprised, as the word means fair.

"When we first called them that, it was just a joke," the Macho explained. "But the nickname stuck and now they even use it amongst themselves."

A little further up we came to a group of Negroes and our guide told the Macho to stop. He then enquired where the princess could be found.

"She's down at the river washing clothes."

They told us exactly where we would find her. At the river we left the car by a bridge and went off on foot, our guide leading us upstream along a complicated path. Sometimes, to avoid getting our feet wet, we had to jump from stone to stone. Sometimes we had to crawl under branches which hung down into the water. Finally our guide stopped and pointed to the princess who, naturally, was just like any other Negress.

She didn't stop washing to talk to us. At first she seemed a bit reserved, but that no doubt was only shyness, for when she had got used to us she opened up readily. When we asked about her royal father she fairly beamed.

"It used to be so beautiful," she said, "when we had a *fiesta*. He used to be carried round on a gilded throne, dressed in scarlet and with a glittering crown. He was carried everywhere, down every street, so that everybody could see him."

The memory of it gladdened her. We asked why no one had succeeded him.

"The *Rubios* would like someone chosen from our family, but none of my brothers wants to take it on."

She was silent for a moment, then added:

"We shall never have a king again . . . never . . . never."

We left the sad princess to her reveries of bygone splendours.

.   .   .   .   .

In the hall of the hotel, when we got back, Aramayo ran into a friend of his, a certain Don Enrique, to whom he explained the object of our visit.

"I own a *finca* near here," said Don Enrique, "and most of the farm hands are Blacks. Let me tell you a story. An old man who was almost past working came to me a little time ago and said: 'You ought to beat the Negroes. You're much too soft with them.'

" 'But you're one yourself,' I answered.

" 'What? Me black!' he exclaimed. 'Look at this.'

"He rolled up one of his sleeves.

" 'Do you see that white spot?' he asked.

"There was indeed a pale patch about the size of a pigeon's egg.

" 'That's my real colour,' he said. 'All the rest of my skin has got tanned by the sun. So you see I'm not really a Negro at all.' "

We tried to understand these black people of the Yungas and why they should have adopted Aymara customs.

Generally Negroes gravitate to a form of civilization nearer to our own, but here, although having a choice, they had adopted a form even more archaic than that of their ancient masters. Of course, in Africa, Negroes see the material advantages of white civilization and they either take it over to a point where they forget their own ancestral traditions, or else eschew it altogether and continue their own 'unmechanized' existence. More rarely, they may adopt it for a time, and then revert to the old order. Here, however, the situation had been rather different. The one-time slaves found themselves in sympathy with the workers—the Indians—rather than with their European overlords.

. . . . .

At two o'clock the following afternoon we said good-bye to Aramayo on the station platform at La Paz. In a few hours we should be at Guaqui. The next day we should be in Peru.

The first person we met on the train was a priest who was a friend of the *padrecito* who had been so hospitable to us in Jesus de Machaca.

"I don't suppose you know," he said, "but the *padrecito* has had to leave his parish. He tried to stop the Indians dancing in the church. They turned on him and even threatened his life. He's with us now, in the monastery at Guaqui."

XI

Cuzco

ARRIVING at Lima after an uneventful journey we at once began to make plans for our researches in Peru, calling on various authorities, particularly with a view to cadging means of transport.

Though our principal objectives were the Cholone and Jibito Indians living in the forests on the left bank of the Huallaga, we wanted, if our finances would run to it, to squeeze in a trip to Cuzco, ancient capital of the Inca empire. The kind offer of air transport by M. Faucet, manager of the aviation company, made it possible.

The other part of our programme, which we were beginning to be seriously worried about, was greatly facilitated by an invitation from the manager of the French mines at Huaron. The mines being situated near Cerro de Pasco, they offered a convenient halt on the way to Tingo Maria, a small town on the Huallaga below which the river is navigable by rafts.

But first of all to Cuzco. A little before dawn we were at the aerodrome ready to embark. When we were called forward by loud speaker we found ourselves gathering in a group with some Americans from the States (easily recognizable), a priest, and three nuns in fluttering white head-dresses.

The sun rose on mountains of soft outline as we flew over the arid coastal zone, whose grey soil would be fertile if only it could receive some rain. Never a drop: to get any water at all, wells a hundred and fifty feet deep have to be dug.

The plane climbed up and up. The air hostess came round telling us to use our oxygen apparatus. I felt like having a nap, but she wouldn't let me. Sleeping was forbidden at a height of 23,000 feet.

The four-hour flight was soon over. The plane lost height circling round and round in a spiral, as there wasn't enough elbow room for it to come down on the straight, for Cuzco lies at the bottom of a narrow basin. The approach was as beautiful as one could imagine.

At Cuzco, as at Copacabana, we were really on the spree, and we were determined to make the most of it. We began, of course, with a stroll round the town—a town of varying colour, predominant being the blue grey of the Inca buildings and the tawny pink of the Spanish

128

The Market at Cuzco

Machu Pichu

churches; an imperial city, like Potosi, but at the same time a colonial one by virtue of its religious architecture, with doorways flanked by spiral pillars embossed with twisting vines, carved in a stone of deep pink like grapes in September.

"There's sure to be a main square somewhere, Jean-Luc," I said as we prowled around, "with a tidy little public garden and a band-stand. That's inescapable."

I was right, and when we came to it, there was a coloured statue of an Indian with three feathers in his thick hair which stood in the centre facing the cathedral. The great walls of the cathedral, bare, rust-coloured, stretched along the whole of one side. All of Seville, Segovia, and Toledo was there, combining in this dream of a new Spain. Cuzco probably marks the zenith of this spiritual exportation.

But on the heels of Christopher Columbus came Pizarro and others, who sacked, looted, and burned, who were greedy for gold. The last emperor offered a roomful of the precious metal as high as his hand could reach, and they promised to spare his life. He did more: he embraced the Christian faith.

But the Inca only fanned their greed when he said:

"I can fill this room with gold and you can take it; you can take all you can lay your hands on in Cuzco. Add to that what you have already and it's still only a drop in the ocean."

These unlucky words were to cost him his life. Convinced that the gold they coveted could not escape them now, the conquerors put the Inca to death, but it was a case of killing the goose that laid the golden eggs. With the death of the Inca the precious metal became elusive, the sources whence it came dried up, the fabulous treasure disappeared. Today one can still read and hear tales of it, and these must surely have some factual basis.

The revenue which had formerly flowed automatically into the Inca's treasury had now to be searched for: the conquerors had to exchange the easy chair of the tax collector for the pick of the mining pioneer.

And now we were standing on the very spot which had witnessed the chief events of this extraordinary story.

From the main square in which these sombre thoughts were forced on us, we went off in search of the Temple of the Sun, at once the grandest and most venerable relic of the Inca empire. We were familiar with the descriptions of the early chroniclers, but knew that the Spaniards had destroyed the ancient temples and used their stones

I

to build their churches, also that in 1950 a great earthquake had ravaged Cuzco and its surroundings; so we wondered what we should find of the splendours of the past.

The former Temple had faced east to greet the rising sun. It had been covered with a thatched roof. Its four walls had been inlaid with gold from top to bottom and on the high altar the face of the sun had been carved in a single sheet of that metal, with flames radiating outwards. This had been the only image in the temple, but on either side of it the embalmed bodies of dead kings sat on thrones of gold. Only the Emperor Huaina-Capac faced the sun, he being the wisest, the most courageous, and the most pious of all the Incas.

Around this temple, five great pavilions of pyramidal form were dedicated to other heavenly bodies. First of all one to the Moon, wife of the Sun. She had the features of a woman and the walls of her temple were white. One was to Venus, page of the Sun, but the Pleiades and all the other deities were thought to be in the sky to wait not on the Sun but on the Moon, which was quite reasonable really since they were only seen at night. There were temples, too, to the Lightning and the Thunder, but these, as was proper, were the servants of the Sun. Lastly there was a temple to the Rainbow whose colours were reproduced on plaques of gold.

When the Indians of old had seen a rainbow they had promptly shut their mouths and for greater surety had clapped their hands to them. Had they neglected this precaution their teeth would have decayed.

We turned off to the right of the square and went down a narrow street with iron-grey stone walls. The rectangular stones seemed to be stuck together. We knew the Incas never used cement. We also knew that they didn't know the use of steel for facing stone, yet it would have been impossible to introduce the blade of a knife into the cracks.

"The earthquake doesn't seem to have done much damage," I said. "They haven't budged an inch."

"That is true enough," replied Jean-Luc, "but try looking a little higher than your own nose."

The spectacle there was very different, for the upper part of the walls was of Spanish construction and looked as though it had been under shell fire.

The ground before us ran gently down to a little stream. Stopping, we noticed on our left on a slight elevation a great rounded wall.

"There you are! Do you recognize the tribune from which the priests used to address the people?"

"Yes. Let's go and have a look."

There, too, Inca building had stood the test of time and earthquake, though the walls and tower of the Spanish church erected above it were in ruins.

We went into the temple, where a guide led us through a maze of ancient walls, divided up still further by modern partitions. We were quite lost. It was impossible to form any idea of the original plan of the building. A half-ruined cloister raised its bits of wall in the middle of ancient masonry.

"Where's the Temple of the Moon?" we asked.

"Behind you. We'll look at it presently. First of all we'll see the church which has replaced the Temple of the Sun."

When we entered the church we were aghast. The earthquake had returned it to its former god, the Sun. The roof had gone, and the sunshine struck down between the truncated pillars of the Christian sanctuary. There had been no attempt to clear up the mess: velvet hangings fringed with gold lay on the ground mixed up with bits of painted or sculptured wood. It looked as though a horde of savages had sacked the place.

The guide, seeing our astonishment, thought we could not have heard of the earthquake.

"It was terrible," he said. "I was standing in the cathedral square when I heard what sounded like underground thunder. Then the earth started heaving beneath my feet. I was like an eggshell rolling on a plate. Everything began to fall, the chimneys first, then the walls. In a trice the town was one vast heap of debris. There were other shocks later, but the first was much the worst. After the first panic was over, we could see that some houses were still standing. All of them damaged, though. Some of them suddenly came down several days later when nobody expected it. Others, though cracked, could be repaired and strengthened by wooden piers bolted to the masonry. But you see how well the Incas understood their business. Their walls held all right. . . . The Indians here say an earthquake comes every three hundred years. It's true there was one three centuries ago, but further back than that it's impossible to go. The Incas recorded their dates with *quipus* and we don't know how to read them."

Quipus are knotted strings arranged according to some complicated scheme to which we have no key. Each arrangement had its meaning.

There are scholars, however, who deny that the Incas had any form of writing at all, and it's impossible to say anything definite on this subject. An enormous number of *quipus* were destroyed by the Spaniards or in the great fires at the time when Atahualpa, the last Inca, was murdered, or again in the numerous upheavals in the centuries which followed.

"What was that long wall we followed, coming here from the main square?"

"That was the convent of the Virgins of the Sun, the *ñustas*."

Where the apse of the church should have been we found the enormous stones of Inca masonry much easier to examine, for they had become completely freed from the Spanish superstructure. They were beautifully faced and polished. Climbing up onto some, we found ourselves looking down on a whole quarter of Cuzco. We were at the summit of the tribune of the priests which we had noticed from outside.

We went down into a little crypt, also of Inca origin, directly above which the Spaniards had erected their high altar. A lead coffin was there.

"Whose is it?" we asked.

"Some descendant's of the conquistadors. We don't know whose."

Retracing our steps, we again crossed the cloister and entered the Temple of the Moon, then that of the Stars. They were small rectangular chapels whose walls were scooped out in little niches, in which, said our guide, the priests used to lay their offerings.

We didn't feel any ill effects from the altitude—Cuzco is 12,000 feet up—but the heat was oppressive. Our mouths were parched and we decided we needed a glass of beer before going off to explore the native market, situated near the station.

On our way we passed another wall of polished stone, and inquired of a passing priest what it was.

"It used to contain the Inca's garden," came the answer. "It was there that the Emperor used to plough the first furrow to open the ploughing season officially. In one corner of it were life-sized reproductions in gold of every plant and animal in his empire. The whole garden was a kind of religious cult, and it was believed that as long as it was perfectly kept up the crops would be good, the forests vigorous, and animals plentiful for the hunter."

The market was full of life. Indian women, squatting cross-legged on the ground, sold fruit, vegetables, trinkets, and objects with magic

Machu Pichu.
Main Sanctuary

Machu Pichu. Observatory and Phallic Temple

properties for the use of sorcerers. Blind beggars played harsh music on a sort of saw. Men driving llamas had obviously just come in from the neighbouring country. Tourists, mostly from the States, were buying *ponchos*, *lluchos*, shawls, and blankets. Ragged children rushed about, calling out in piping voices. According to the historians children of Inca days had a harsh upbringing and their descendants at least resembled them in that.

If a mother, on some exceptional occasion, wanted to demonstrate her affection, she took water into her mouth and spat it all over her little one's body, except the top of the head, which she never touched. She never nursed her baby in her arms, but always kept it in its cradle, a hollow in the ground padded with old rags, where it was given various toys to play with. She only suckled it three times a day, and even then didn't pick it up, but lay on top of it. Until it was weaned, she kept away from the husband because his company would have turned the milk and made the child rickety.

When we returned to our hotel we were in pensive mood. Though so little was left of it, we had so to speak glimpsed the grandeur of the past, and were able to imagine the city of two hundred thousand souls which it had been, with palaces encrusted with gold, and priests and dignitaries in gorgeous clothes.

Next morning we went off with an official guide to visit the environs. Our presence had been reported in the local newspaper and on the wireless, and everyone was anxious to be of service to us.

Our first objective was the fortresses surrounding the town, the most remarkable and justly celebrated of which is Sacsahuaman. Its enormous stones were quite different from what we had seen so far, each block being 3,000 cubic feet and heaven knows how many tons. Though unsymmetrical, they fitted each other perfectly, and once again we couldn't have inserted a razor blade into the cracks. Our guide told us of a sort of historical pageant that had been organized, in which he had taken the part of the Inca. Taking us to the edge of the valley from which one could look down on the whole of Cuzco, he said:

"Do you know the legend about the origin of Cuzco?"

We didn't and, sitting down on some stones by the roadside, we listened to his story.

"Long before the Incas got here, this region was inhabited by savage tribes. They worshipped plants and animals, the mountains and the elements. They performed human sacrifices, cutting open the chests of women and children and tearing out the heart and lungs.

"In those days there was nothing here but the mountains and their shrubs and bushes. These people lived in caves, some of them under the ground. Without either laws or religion, they were no better than animals; they mated promiscuously, having no institution of marriage.

"They fed on wild grasses, roots, and fruit. They were also cannibals.

"Then," said the guide, becoming lyrical, "our brother, the Sun, moved by compassion, sent down as messengers two of his children, a son and a daughter. He sent them down from the sky to the shores of Lake Titicaca, telling them to teach men to adore him as their god. Also to give them laws, teach them to till the soil and breed animals, to spin wool and weave it into stuffs.

"He gave them a golden rod two fingers thick and five fingers long, and said: 'Wherever this rod sticks into the ground, there must you stop and found a kingdom.'

"So off they went and wandered about, but the rod didn't stick in the ground till at noon they came to a place to sleep. Then suddenly the rod plunged into the ground and disappeared.

"The son was the first Inca, the daughter the first queen. Though brother and sister, they were also man and wife. The Inca said: 'It is in this little valley that our father the Sun wishes us to gather men and teach them.' On that, each set out, the prince to the North, the princess to the South. They combed the bushes and the mountain caves, gathering men.

"They brought them here and made a town of two parts. The Inca founded Upper Cuzco, the Queen, Lower Cuzco. Though divided into two parts all men were to be as brothers. Only, those in Upper Cuzco were to be the elder brothers. And ever since that time our towns and villages have always been divided into two parts.

"The Inca taught men to plough and sow seeds. The Queen taught spinning and weaving and how to make clothes. And when they were taught, the Indians went off to bring in others, who believed their story when they saw the clothes they wore."

We were silent for a while; then the guide shook us from our dreams of the past by taking a box of matches from his pocket.

"Look," he said. "A ñusta—a Virgin of the Sun."

On the box, in bright colours, was a picture of a girl in a dancing posture, her hands held out to a red sun. She seemed to be saying:

"And my eyes can bear to gaze
Upon the sacred sun from which I stem."

But the Virgins of the Sun had gone, ravished by the conquerors or escaped to some inaccessible fastness on the confines of the empire.

We got to our feet and started down towards an amphitheatre nearby. The stage consisted of an enormous rock in the middle of which was a gaping crevice about one yard wide.

"This is the Temple of Love," said our guide. "Certain marriages were celebrated here—and consummated. The priests stood on the walls of the amphitheatre. The couples climbed on to the stone block where they received the sacrament. The rest took place inside the rock."

We entered into the crevice which formed a sort of corridor, giving access to rooms on either side, hollowed out of the rock. In the rooms were stone beds and above were holes which served as chimneys. We climbed up onto the top of the rock which formed a platform of rough surface and pitted with holes of natural origin. At one edge where the stone curled up a seat had been cut. In front of it was a hole in which sacrifices had been made—perhaps human sacrifices—on the side of which a serpent was sculptured in intaglio. And from the serpent water flowed. Doubly symbolic. For the serpent always represents sex; so does water. Here was the union of feminine water with the serpent of male sexuality.

After inspecting the remains of other Inca temples—they were to be met with at every turn—we went back to the centre of the town. We wanted to take things easy, as we were to make an early start next morning for Machu-Pichu.

Woken up long before dawn, we joined the group of upwards of a dozen tourists gathered in the hall of the hotel. Most of them came from the States, the most striking being a middle-aged woman who spoke sometimes in French, sometimes in Spanish, but chiefly in English. We never knew her by any other name than Evelyn. She had been all over South America, accompanying her husband, who travelled on business. While he saw to his affairs in the various capitals, she would dash off in all directions to see all there was to see, whether of archaeological or ethnic interest, or merely scenery. Having bought an Indian costume the previous day, she was sporting it already, the flaming scarlet bodice making her pink complexion even lighter by contrast and turning her grey hair to snow. She was gaiety itself, and was talking eagerly to two or three girls. We tacked ourselves on to the group and shared a taxi with them to the station, where the rail-car awaited us.

This was a small motor coach mounted on railway wheels. There was no road to Machu-Pichu and the terrain there made the construction of an airfield impossible. Faster than a train, the rail-car made the double journey possible in a day, so that we avoided spending a night at the little hotel that had been built near the ruins.

The line ran along the Urubamba, sacred river of the Incas, after crossing a mountain pass which had been negotiated in the most curious way. The line zigzagged back and forth up the slope, and, as there was no room for the construction of even hairpin bends, the car had to go forwards up one leg, backwards up the next.

The Urubamba was enclosed by steep walls covered by vegetation, so steep that we soon got cricks in our necks gazing upwards at the mountain tops. The rattle of the car discouraged conversation. After about five hours it stopped and the conductor told us to get out. Two small vans were waiting for us.

"There you are," said a man. "That's Machu-Pichu by the side of that sugar-loaf mountain. You can see the ruins from here."

But we could only see the sugar-loaf mountain, which shot up sheer above the valley. Of the ruins we could distinguish nothing.

It took us half an hour to reach them. Then we were put down in front of the small building which served as hotel. We had a rapid lunch there on the terrace outside in a blaze of sunshine, then went to see the ruins. Not such ruins either. Much better preserved than anything we had seen either at Cuzco or in Bolivia. Tucked away in this remote spot this huge building had escaped the Spaniards' hands. Indeed it was only discovered in 1926.

We at once noticed two styles, or rather two methods of construction, the one with rectangular faced stones perfectly fitting, the other with rough uneven stones gripping each other by means of their irregularities; this second method is in no way original, having been employed in pretty well every country of the world. The agglomeration of buildings was so vast that we thought it best to follow the guide; also because many of the ruins were no more interesting than those one might find in France—in the Gard or the Basses-Alpes for instance. He explained to us that Machu-Pichu was divided into three quarters, noble, religious, and military. All round were semicircular terraces which, he said, had formerly been cultivated.

"But how could they grow anything on them?" asked Jean-Luc. "Terraced land required irrigation."

"That's right," replied the guide, "but in Inca days irrigation existed. Don't you see those gulleys and conduits? The water used to run everywhere. If there's none now, it's because the spring dried up."

There are two theories about the abandonment of the place. Some say it was the exhaustion of a spring which caused it, or perhaps the absence of rain over several seasons, while others maintain that the population was wiped out by an epidemic. If that was the case, it is surprising that only one skull has ever been found there, that of a girl, a Virgin of the Sun maybe. Indeed there is a legend that a hundred of the virgins, accompanied by some of the women of the royal family, took refuge here at the time of the fall of Cuzco. But that, of course, is mere hearsay.

"Machu-Pichu," said the guide, "was first of all a fortress."

That surprised us, and we couldn't help arguing about it. Why should such an enormous stronghold have been built in a place where a much smaller one would have sufficed? Besides, we had been impressed by the size of the religious quarter, with its many temples. The presence of an observatory, too, pointed to other than military purposes. Possibly it had been a fortress in the first place, and acquired a religious importance subsequently.

The observatory was on top of one of the temples. In the middle was a sundial whose style was a phallus. There was a complicated system of loop-holes, through which the stars could be observed and the seasons calculated. To this day the sun at its solstice strikes a certain stone.

After we had been all round, we went back to the observatory. Some of the American girls were there, one of whom, naïvely sitting on the phallus, was having her photograph taken.

Evening fell. On our right, the huge sugar loaf was invested with a peculiar sheen by the last horizontal rays of the sun. Joining us, the guide said:

"Up there was the last stronghold of all and it, too, had an observatory."

No. Military expediency was certainly not the be-all and end-all of this isolated place hidden in the mountains. Buried in the stones here was some religious secret.

We went down again to the little hotel. On our way, we noticed that the caretaker's house was also of Inca construction. He had only had to put on a thatched roof to restore the building to its primitive state and make a habitable dwelling of it.

·   ·   ·   ·   ·

The next day was devoted to Ollentay Tambo, a fortress, over which hangs a legend as popular as the *Chanson de Roland* is with us.

This trip was by taxi. The driver had brought his son along with him, a little boy whom he had to bring up himself, as his wife had left him.

Up hill and down dale, the road to Ollentay Tambo was magnificent. From Cuzco downwards the climate grew more and more balmy. As in the Puna district near Potosi, eucalyptus trees were scattered about everywhere, filling the sunshine with their scent.

The fortress of Ollentay Tambo stood high over a little village of the same name, most of whose houses dated from the Incas; the walls were formed of the huge stones with which we were now familiar. The people and their costumes were in harmony with the architecture of their ancestors. The narrow streets emptied as we approached, only a few inquisitive children running in our wake. The main street, almost straight, led off from a small square in which two or three shopkeepers stood in front of the shops on the watch for customers. We drove down this street, forded a little stream, and came to a halt on the sand and stones of the opposite bank under the adobe wall which enclosed the precincts of the fortress.

The first thing we had to do was to shake off the crowd of little importuners who wanted to show us round. The fortress was built on a hump jutting out from the mountain-side, and dominated the valley. The slopes had been laid out in terraces, divided in the middle by flights of steps running straight up to where the buildings began. Clinging to the mountain-side, these were in the same style as those of Machu-Pichu. The walls of the keep had gone in many places, but it was easy to reconstruct its general form. Here and there were observation posts, and loopholes through which the Inca archers had shot their flint-headed arrows.

On our left a steep flight of steps led to the religious quarter. Here the workmanship was finer; the stones seemed to have been polished, but once again it was their enormous size which struck us most forcibly—and their beautiful tawny pink colour. The temple was surrounded by stone-built terraces, in the walls of which frequent niches had been scooped out, as at the Temple of the Sun at Cuzco, to receive the offerings made to the gods. One side of the religious quarter was flush with a cliff.

"It didn't need to be guarded on that side," said Jean-Luc. "No one could have scaled that wall."

"Have you noticed," I asked, "that these stones weren't quarried here? The granite of the mountain is a deeper colour."

"They certainly didn't spare themselves any pains, the chaps who built these walls. How they handled these blocks of stone at all is a mystery—and they may have brought them from far afield."

It was our chauffeur who told us the story of Ollentay—of the wicked general who ran off with a *ñusta*, but for greater accuracy we will give here the account given by Ricardo Palma in his *Tradiciones Peruanas*.

In the reign of Pachacutec, the ninth Inca, lived a man called Ollentay, who was *curaca* of Ollentay Tambo besides being commander-in-chief of the army. Becoming the lover of Cusicoylor, one of the Virgins of the Sun, he asked Pachacutec for her hand in marriage in reward for his many services to the crown. This was refused by the proud monarch because she was of royal blood, which, according to the laws of the empire, must never be mixed with that of any family which did not descend directly from Manco Capac. Thereupon the fond *curaca* escaped from Cuzco, taking his mistress with him.

For five years the Inca was unable to subdue the rebel, who had shut himself up in the fortress of Ollentay Tambo. Then another of the Inca's generals, a certain Rumiñahui, convinced his master during a secret interview that what couldn't be got by force could be got by guile and treachery. A plan was concocted. Rumiñahui was thrown into gaol, accused of having violated the sanctuary of the Virgins of the Sun. Stripped of all his dignities, he was publicly flogged into the bargain. Then he was allowed to escape. Reaching Ollentay, he offered his services to the rebel general, who saw in him another victim of oppression. A fellow general, too. Naturally he fell into the trap and gave the new-comer his confidence. Everything worked according to plan, and Rumiñahui was able to deliver the fortress, whose defenders were put to death.

Told amidst those ruins, this love story came to life. It is a well-known story, which has been made the subject of a tragedy often played in Peru, sometimes in Spanish, sometimes in Quechua. The play is widely believed to have come down from Inca times. It was really written by a Spanish priest in 1780, but the truth makes little headway against popular tradition.

Jean-Luc took some photographs and we went back to our taxi. We returned by a different road, passing through Pisac, where we made a brief halt.

A small village with a fortress perched up on the top of a hill which was high enough to damp any desire to climb. Instead, we wandered along the narrow paved lanes which radiated from the little square, whose neglected church was roofless. The houses were miserable. The villagers lived on the product of the soil, selling their wares every Sunday in the market, which was sufficiently picturesque to draw tourists over from Cuzco.

.   .   .   .   .

The next day we flew back to Lima, where we arrived in time for lunch. After lunch we made preparations to leave for Huaron, to which we were to set off very early the following morning.

The train which took us there began climbing almost at once, as the coastal plain is very narrow. Soon we were back in a mountain landscape with the same vegetation as on the Altiplano—the short grass on which the llamas graze. The line we were on is the highest railway in the world. In a few hours, across bridges and through tunnels, it reaches 16,000 feet. Passengers often find it difficult to stand the height and a steward with oxygen is in constant attendance. It didn't bother us at all.

At Huaron a car was waiting for us, and a quarter of an hour later we were at the mine. All arrangements had been made for our stay and after dinner we were taken to a house where a room had been prepared for us.

We slept splendidly at the height of Mont Blanc, though as a matter of fact we were sufficiently tired to have slept anywhere.

"Don't you think," I said next morning, "that leaving air travel out, the faster a journey is the more it tires you? Think of that restful journey we had plodding up the Beni!"

"True enough!"

Doorway at Ollentay-Tambo

Lamista Indians

The Rio Maya

"For my part I'd sooner do twenty-five miles on foot than spend five hours in a train."

"Or take tennis. I've played for hours on end without being half so tired as by a train journey."

This conversation was interrupted by the arrival of an engineer from the mine, a Frenchman, who came to fetch us. Though glad enough to have a glimpse of the highest French mine in the world, we were neither of us keen to study it in detail.

On our way we asked a few questions.

"What metals do you find here?"

"Lead, silver, copper, and zinc. The price of zinc is so low these days that we don't attempt to sell it. We let the stock accumulate hoping for better times."

"Are there any mines still higher up?"

"Certainly. But not many. . . . In France we think in terms of Mont Blanc. People would hardly believe one could lead an everyday life at a height like this."

Once again we were rigged out in miners' kit, and soon we were in the galleries. So long as we were on the level, we didn't feel the altitude at all, but if our guide asked us to climb up a ladder from one gallery to another, we found it most uncomfortable both to move and breathe. The confined atmosphere contributed something to our discomfort, though the mines of Huaron were far better ventilated than those of the Cerro Rico at Potosi.

After lunch we took leave of the engineer and started off again, this time by car, our destination being Cerro de Pasco, the most important town of the region. We arrived in the evening, and at once enquired about a motor coach to Huanuco, which we had to pass through to reach Tingo Maria. We found one at once, the usual bone-shaker of a *gondola*, like the one that had taken us to Copacabana.

Soon after leaving Cerro de Pasco we noticed a group of ruined houses amongst which were several mills. When the Spaniards came, they had used the water-power of the stream to grind the silver ore, abundant in that region. We were to drive along a deep valley, that of the Huallaga. Here it was only a mountain torrent that had gushed out of the Eastern slope of the Andes; further down it would join the Marañon to become an important tributary of the Amazon.

The following day we found another *gondola* to take us on to Tingo Maria. Before it left we had time to wander about the town. The population of Huanuco consists of Quechuas and half-castes. Otherwise we found the town—with its main square planted with trees and equipped with a bandstand—much like any other we had seen.

The *gondola* gradually filled up, then started off. Soon we reached the edge of the forest. We followed the Huallaga, but sometimes the valley narrowed to a gorge in which there was no room for a road. Then we had to climb lateral valleys and go over passes, some of which were over 13,000 feet up.

We were pleased to be back in the forest, which we had got to know in the Beni. Of course it was different here, as we were still in the mountains, but the luxuriance of the dark green vegetation was the same. We thought of the immense labour that was needed for a road in such country, and not only in its construction: a neglected road is soon swallowed up by the forest.

We stopped at a village for lunch, then resumed our journey. When we finally rejoined the Huallaga after the last pass, it was a roaring river rushing down a narrow ravine. Soon we were at Tingo Maria, a town much like any other of tropical America—long straight streets at right angles to one another. It would be hard to imagine a more beautiful situation, at the centre of a round plain ringed by high mountains. The plain was cut in two by the Huallaga along the banks of which the town had been built. Having come down the right bank of the river, the road crossed it here, to strike off to Pucalpa in the West, lying on the Ucayali. From here downstream, the Huallaga is navigable by *balsa*, and that is how most goods are transported to the lower reaches.

We put up at a hotel which had formerly been Swiss, but now was incorporated in a remarkable hotel organization run by the Peruvian government. This establishment at Tingo Maria was certainly an excellent advertisement of it; it consisted of a central building surrounded by huts of wood and wire gauze, each containing two rooms and a bathroom. This dispersion made for coolness and quiet, and the place was most restful. The river ran past only a few yards away, and we were surrounded by green lawns and aromatic trees, the haunt of humming-birds.

We couldn't stay more than a couple of days, however, for we had to push on with our researches. We were impatient to gather information respecting the Cholones and the Jibitos.

In South America *cholo* is the word for a half-caste. Confusion between this and the name of the tribe had been the cause of a little misunderstanding in our case.

The day of our departure from Dunkirk, when we were getting our baggage on board the *Alain Louis-Dreyfus*, we were handed a telegram from friends in Paris asking us to ring them up.

We did so, and learnt that some Peruvian newspapers had launched a campaign against us. According to them we were coming to Peru to study the *cholos*, an intervention as absurd as it was uncalled for. We were taken for ignorant busy-bodies and accused of having openly declared that we knew no more than thirty-three words of the *cholos'* language (which of course is none other than Spanish) picked up from a German professor. They were referring to Professor Tessmann.

Out of this silly misunderstanding, quite a serious affair had been concocted, and various *démentis*, put out without our knowledge by well-intentioned but misinformed people, only made matters worse.

A telegram from us, which we asked the French authorities to confirm, quickly put matters to rights, however, and we forgot all about the incident until, at Lima, we were shown a cartoon which had accompanied one of the protesting articles. We found it very funny. It depicted a handful of French passengers arriving in a small boat at Callao (the port of Lima) scrutinizing the distant coast and exclaiming: "But where are the cannibals?"

This anecdote will suffice to show how jealous the Peruvians are of their good name in the world. And they have every justification for being so.

At Tingo Maria, after drawing a lot of blanks, we finally ran to earth a tailor who had come originally from Lamas. He had left his birthplace sixteen years earlier but he was still able to speak of the Cholones as people he had known well. Of the Jibitos, on the other hand, he had never even heard.

So we had at last got on the track of one of these two tribes. We decided to leave for Lamas as soon as we got back to Lima, and we jumped into the next available plane.

On our return to the capital we received a message asking us to call as soon as possible at the editorial office of one of the newspapers. Shades of that earlier misunderstanding gave rise to a moment's uneasiness. There was no call for it: the newspaper in question merely wanted to interview us, and the same journalists who were once holding us up to public obloquy now became our friends.

XII

Lamas

WE flew to Tarapoto, a typical small town quite close to Lamas, situated just to the east of the mountains in the low-lying region of tropical forest known as the Montaña. Chinese dozed behind their counters in the shops of the main square; otherwise the population was of half-castes. In the evening the girls disported themselves in bright cotton frocks, yellow, orange, green, with no sleeves or shoulders.

We had letters of introduction which paved our way and we were soon to make the acquaintance of Don Pancho, a government expert in production statistics, a man in the forties, and a *cholo*. Like most Peruvians of the Montaña he had a coppery complexion, though his features reminded one at times of the Spanish *hidalgo*. When not busy on government work, he eked out his slender salary by trading in cotton and coffee. We made friends at once.

"You're looking for Cholones and Jibitos," he said, "and someone's put you on to Lamas. You may be on the right track, but I, for one, have never so much as heard of them. . . . Now look here—I'm off on a round tomorrow: if you like, come with me. I can easily make it my business to pass through Lamas. If you find what you're after, you can stay there. Otherwise you can come on with me through the forest, questioning the Indians as you go."

Of course we jumped at the suggestion. Don Pancho had no car at his disposal, so it was in another jolting *gondola* that we drove off on the following morning along a rough track, fording streams and ploughing through forest and mud. Presently we began to climb, the *gondola* jolting and lurching more than ever. For nearly an hour we had been climbing when Don Pancho pointed to some roofs on the top of a hill.

"Lamas."

Nor was this town different in any essential from another. A church, some trees growing in the clay soil of the square, a few straight streets, one or two Chinese shopkeepers, a club, a wireless blaring dance tunes on the square at night. Don Pancho introduced us to the Sub-Prefect, a stout genial man who at once took us to the club for a glass of beer and promised to do all he could to assist us during our stay.

San Miguel

Tabaloso

Quetchua girl

Don Pancho then took us to a building in the main street.

"I want you to meet the school inspector and his secretary," he said. "They know a lot about the Indians and may well be able to help you."

It was thus that we made the acquaintance of Guillermo Rios and his assistant, whom we were soon to be calling by his Christian name, Arquimedes. Neither of them had heard of the Cholones or the Jibitos. We decided therefore to spend the next few days studying the people here, then push on with Don Pancho into the 'interior' to see if we could find any trace of the two tribes we were in search of.

Surrounded by tropical forests Lamas seemed to us like the place of one's dreams. The delicious climate was exempt from all excesses, the altitude (something under 3,000 feet) nicely balancing the latitude.

Next morning we explored the town thoroughly, finding out the names of the various Indian quarters and mapping them out.

The centre was inhabited by the half-castes, who had come from elsewhere, for the Lamista Indians never mix their blood. The half-caste quarters nevertheless bore Indian names, except one, Calvario. The others were Muniches, Ankoallo, Suchiche, Killolpa. These quarters ran into each other without any visible boundaries.

Surrounding these were the Indian quarters: Salas, Sangamas, Ichuizas, Shupingahuas, Amasifuen, Pashanases, Tupullimas, Guerras. In these, in spite of the proximity of white civilization, the native traditions remained untouched.

The names of the quarters were the names of clans. Every Indian bore the surname of his quarter.

The half-castes we talked to told us the Indians spoke Quechua, which we found some difficulty in believing, for we were very far removed from the area of distribution of that language. We wondered whether the word wasn't used loosely here, and applied indiscriminately to any Indian tongue. We referred the matter to Arquimedes, who was a native of the place.

"Yes," he said, "they do speak Quechua, but it's not the same as the language spoken at Cuzco. This is the old Quechua such as was spoken in Inca days, or perhaps it would be more accurate to say that they are two branches of the same language which have undergone a different evolution."

"But in a region where so many different languages are spoken, how did it come about that Quechua gained such a hold? The Incas may well have known of this country, but it never came under their sway."

K

In answer to that, we were referred to the work of Dr. Pedro Weiss. In this author's *Estudio Sobre los Lamistas*, he says as follows on the supposed origin of this people:

> In Inca history, during the confused period of Yarhuarhuaca and Viracocha, we are told of a revolt of the proud tribes of the Chancas, under the leadership of their *curaca*. In their advance, the Chancas came dangerously close to Cuzco, threatening the very heart of the Empire. They were defeated, however, in the famous battle of Yahuarpampa, a town whose very stones (so legend tells) rose to defend their Emperor.
>
> The Chancas, though pardoned, could not bear to be regarded as a defeated people, and they and their chiefs moved off down the Huallaga valley.
>
> These events are supposed to have taken place a hundred and fifty years before the coming of the Spaniards.
>
> In the Huallaga region the Lamistas are taken for the descendants of the Chancas. The *curaca*, whom the Spaniards would have called *generalissimo*, is said to have settled in the Ankoallo quarter, to which he gave his name.

We are ourselves inclined to give credence to this story, and to regard the language spoken by the Lamistas as proof that they came from Inca country.

Indeed it is probable that this migration followed much the same path as we had taken, passing through Cerro de Pasco and Huanuco, though below Tingo Maria they may well have continued downstream on *balsas*, the river being thenceforward navigable, though by these craft alone on account of the rapids.

A fine epic of the Chancas. When they finally came to a halt they were no doubt attracted by the temperate climate of Lamas. To go further would have been unwise. Coming from the Cordillera they would have found the sticky heat of the lowland forests too enervating. Day and night a cool breeze blew over this hill which was sometimes spoken of as the sanatorium of the Iquitos. A rather strange nickname forsooth, for it would be difficult to imagine a sick person standing the journey to it; nor can one imagine there an institution of any comfort.

At Lamas we worked chiefly on two of the quarters, the Sangamas and the Shupingahuas, whose social structure we wished to discover. Somewhat anxious about our reception, we approached the Indians armed, not merely with our habitual notebooks, but with a little bag of necklaces and bracelets.

At first they held aloof, merely laughing as we passed. At a stream, a group of women were chatting as they did their washing. A band of children followed at a distance, and when we stopped they did the same. Finally curiosity won and they joined us.

"Can you speak Spanish?" we asked the boldest, who seemed older than the others.

"Yes."

"Where do you live?"

"Over there."

He pointed to a group of houses on the hillside.

"Take us there, will you? We'd like to see it."

We wanted to sketch a plan of a typical dwelling. We had already noticed that the door usually opened to the East.

He led the way willingly enough, chattering with the other children. The ice was broken.

Reaching the houses he had pointed to, we saw an old woman who sat spinning, while a little girl turned the wheel.

We asked José, our guide, if the woman was his mother.

"No."

"But isn't this your house?"

"No. That one."

"Aren't your parents there?"

"No. They're in their *chacra*."

As the old woman didn't seem to be scared of us we thought we'd question her.

"José, what's her name?"

"Candelaria Sangama."

We gave her a necklace and bracelet for the little girl. The result was somewhat startling: we were suddenly besieged by families on every side, come to claim from these *amiguitos* one of the treasures from their sack. Until then the place had seemed deserted.

Our bag was rapidly emptied. Another old woman came up carrying a little girl for whom she wanted a necklace, and we were relieved to find there was just one brooch left at the bottom.

Candelaria, devoured by curiosity, was gazing at us.

"May we see your house, Candelaria?"

No answer. She didn't understand Spanish. We looked to José to act as interpreter.

"Ask Candelaria whether we can see her house."

The boy smiled, but said nothing to her. He understood us perfectly, and we had heard him gabbling in Quechua with his companions. This was our first experience of a curious phenomenon in child bilingualism. They can think and speak in two languages, but are quite incapable of translating from one to another.

We jumped to this quickly and asked if there was a man who could speak the two languages.

"Siméon, Siméon," cried the children in chorus.

They ran down the hill and we followed them towards the Shupingahuas quarter, till they stopped in front of a mud house that was unlike any of the others. Siméon at once offered to help us. He was about thirty and had his name tattooed in large letters on his left forearm.

"Where did you learn to speak Spanish like that?"

"In the army. During my military service. What can I do for you?"

"Translate what we say to Candelaria Sangama."

"Certainly, *amiguito*. Let's go."

We went back with him. Candelaria was trying to chase the children away with shouts and threatening gestures. An eighteen-year-old boy, whom we had found with Siméon, had come along too. Tied round his head was a handkerchief folded diagonally with the points upwards. It was a slightly greyish blue with red and yellow flowers embroidered on it. We saw many Lamistas wearing handkerchiefs in this way.

Candelaria spoke to him volubly in Quechua, and the boy took a *machete* and walked away.

"What's the name of your friend?" we asked Siméon.

"Andres Tapullima."

"What's Tapullima mean?"

"It's just a name. He lives in the quarter of the Tapullimas."

"What's your surname, Siméon?"

"I'm Siméon Guerra Sangama."

"But Guerras and Sangamas are both quarters. That means you have two surnames!"

"My mother came from the Guerras, my father from the Sangamas."

In countries that have come under Spanish influence as well as in Spain today the mother's surname is used as well as the father's. We were nevertheless surprised by what he said. We had been told there was no intermarriage between the quarters, even today, and he had been born thirty years before. When we questioned him, however, he failed to enlighten us.

"The old customs are dying out," he said evasively and promptly changed the subject. "What is it you want me to say to Candelaria?"

"We'd like to see her house, and, if she doesn't mind, to make a plan of it."

Siméon spoke to Candelaria, who then turned to us and said: "*Sí.*"

Which, apart from *amiguito*, was probably the only Spanish word she knew.

Siméon came in with us. Just as we were getting down to our work Andres came back with two coconuts. In a somewhat imperious way Candelaria ordered him to cut away the outer husk with his *machete*. That done, he pierced a hole in the tender part of the nut through which it germinates. Candelaria held out a calabash and Andres poured the milk into it and offered it to us. In the heat of the day it seemed cold as ice. The pulp was delicious too.

We began to take stock of the house. The floor was of beaten earth on ground level. The roof was supported by five posts at the back and five in the front, the former being inside the wall, the latter outside. Forked at the top, they carried beams which ran in one piece the length of the building and were secured by strips of bark.

The walls were a lattice of one-inch canes of *palma brava*, lined with strips about sixteen inches wide of plaited palm leaves. A ceiling of *palma brava* ran half the length of the house, providing a loft.

The two front corners were occupied by beds, bamboo mattresses raised up on legs and covered with bands of plaited palm leaves. The beds were screened by white cotton curtains with thin blue stripes.

"Where did those curtains come from?"

"The men weave them."

"Don't the women weave?"

"No. Only men can weave."

The roof was steep, with a palm leaf thatch of up to eight inches in thickness, for rain is both frequent and heavy.

From the roof hung something we had never seen before, an inverted shallow bowl a foot in diameter and four inches deep with a hole in the bottom. A cord passed through the hole and was attached to a wooden toggle which held the bowl up. Another stick, also about four inches long, was thrust through the cord lower down.

We stared at it, trying to guess what purpose it could serve. We had to give up and ask Siméon.

"It's to keep rats and mice away," he said.

The furniture was rudimentary: the beds, two benches, and a stool, a round platter of wood against the back wall, on which the maize was pounded, and two round stones to pound it with. For the rest, a lot of earthenware vessels called *cantaros* (fifteen of them) and several baskets, all stood on the ground. One of the vessels, a good yard in diameter, was the *cantaro a chicha*, which is a beer made from maize.

A smaller vessel, held up from the ground by a three-pronged forked post, was covered by a cloth tied down.

"That's for keeping clothes in," Siméon told us. "Propped up like that, the mice can't get into it."

Other clothes hung from a line stretched across the room, and hanging from the ceiling just above our heads was a deerskin.

At the foot of one of the beds was a heap of raw cotton right up to the ceiling. The cotton-seeds were still in it: you could feel them when you touched the stuff.

By the door, outside the house, stood the spinning wheel. We asked Candelaria to show us how it worked, and she spun a few yards for our benefit. Absorbed in her work, she seemed to forget our presence. We admired the dexterity of her fingers. The little girl turned the wheel, and Candelaria, half backing, half sidling, moved away as the yarn grew longer. Passing a bush, she laid the yarn on it and backed away still further, smiling. At another bush she did the same. And so on from bush to bush till she was quite far away at the end of a series of festoons. We thought of Rimbaud's lines:

> *J'ai tendu des cordes de clocher à clocher, des guirlandes de fenêtre à fenêtre, des chaînes d'or d'étoile à étoile et je danse.*

·   ·   ·   ·   ·

We were now on easy terms with the Indians.

The men wore light trousers of unbleached or beige cotton, often rolled up to their knees, particularly when walking any distance or carrying loads; a shirt, generally sky-blue, thrown back so as to show a wedge of back well below the base of the neck, the opening at the front flanked by a row of buttons on either side. The front itself was often pleated and the garment so short as to leave the midriff bare. On their heads they often had a handkerchief, as has been already described, worn low enough to cover the eyebrows. The hair was cut short, sometimes with a little fringe high on the forehead.

The women wore a long skirt of dark blue cotton, spun, woven, and dyed locally, reminding one of a gipsy's, gathered in at the top by a tape run through the hem. It was tucked up for walking. When at work, at home or in the *chacras*, it was often their only article of clothing. Otherwise they would wear a white blouse embroidered in front with blue and red flowers.

Their long hair was usually done in two plaits. On their heads, they wore cyclamen-coloured kerchiefs tied at the nape, the ends hanging down their backs. They loved necklaces, bracelets, earrings, and brooches. Most of them wore five or six necklaces and many bracelets, made of beads or wild berries. To be given any trinket always delighted them, though we noticed that, when we gave necklaces or bracelets, they would as a rule unstring them and make them up again according to their own taste. And they never grew too old for these adornments. Candelaria Sangama herself came to her *amiguitos* early one morning to ask for a necklace.

The women wore no underclothes, and neither men nor women wore any kind of footwear. It is a sign of nobility to go barefoot and the Lamistas despise those who do not.

These people are meticulously clean. They wash with soap they make themselves from lard and wood-ash. If they've no soap, they crush the berry of a tree called *tingana* and rub themselves all over with the pulp.

Among them we only encountered one case of sickness—a young man who, so far as we could judge, must have been stricken with poliomyelitis, and who dragged himself about with his hands.

Dr. Pedro Weiss, who had taken a great interest in the subject, emphasizes the excellent health they enjoy, and points out that, unlike the half-castes of Lamas, they have very good teeth.

The men we talked to wore bracelets and anklets made of what Siméon told us was iguana-skin.

"Why do they wear them?"

The answer wasn't readily forthcoming.

"Well, Siméon?"

Siméon spoke in Quechua to the others standing by. There was quite a long discussion. Finally, turning to us, he said:

"It's for decoration."

We left it at that for the moment, though we were well aware there was more behind.

Getting on to the subject of illness, we asked how they treated simple wounds.

"If you cut yourself with your *machete*, what do you do?"

"I crush some charcoal and put the powder on the place. Then I tie a rag round it and leave it until it's healed."

Interested in the subject, they volunteered further information.

"For stomach troubles, we rub our stomachs with hot urine, and we drink a cup of urine three times a day, either just as it is or salted."

For eye troubles, the head and face were rubbed every morning for a week with stale urine mixed with certain wild herbs.

For a viper bite, human excrement was left to soak in water which was drunk several times a day. Sometimes for wounds they did the same with cow-dung.

.   .   .   .   .

We were beginning to understand the social organization of the Lamistas. We had quickly recognized the strength of family ties. So long as children, even after marriage, lived with their parents, they bowed to the authority of the head of the house. That authority, on his death, passed to his widow, to whom the eldest son would be subordinate. Both in Siméon's house and Andres's the father reigned supreme. In Candelaria's case no problem could have arisen, as her only descendant was her small granddaughter.

At the same time each family had close bonds with all the other families of the quarter, the whole forming a clan, as with gipsies. Formerly the different quarters were sharply divided, even hostile to one another; now it was difficult to see any sign of enmity between them.

Arquimedes told us that up to a few years previously, during the *fiesta* of Santa Rosa, patron saint of Lamas, there had been serious clashes in the town between groups from different clans, involving dozens of deaths. Those days had gone, leaving only a certain stand-offishness, not unlike the jealousy between neighbouring villages in France.

We found them much less concerned about their relations with one another than with the presence in their midst of whites and half-castes. They were the only Indians of that region that had resisted intermarriage and cultural assimilation. They were jealous of their traditions and determined to hold fast to them.

According to the school inspector, they would refuse to send their children to any school that wasn't reserved exclusively for them. Rather than have their children rubbing shoulders with half-castes they would build a purely Indian school with their own poor savings.

Eager as we were to know all about sorcery, we took our time before cautiously edging up to the subject. Then little by little we accumulated scraps of information which revealed four different categories of sorcerers:

1. *Curanderos*, or healers, were the lowest order.
2. *Hechiceros*, or *pusangueros*, charmers dealing with love and matrimonial issues.
3. *Maleros*, casters of spells.
4. *Magos*, or *advinos*, at the summit of the hierarchy.

To become any one of these, the candidate had to pass through a sort of initiation. First he went to see a *mago*. The *magos*, considered to have attained a state of perfection, were the great initiators of others.

The *mago* takes the candidate to a distant place known to him alone and makes him build a shelter there big enough to sling a hammock in.

The novice has to stay there a year, leaving his hammock as little as possible and observing a rigorous abstinence. During this time the only person he sees is the *mago* who visits him and administers a decoction of a liana called *haya-huasca*.

As he gives his pupil this syrupy liquid, which has the property of giving visions, the *mago* chews a quid of tobacco and chants in Quechua:

Ihanunda mariri,	You will fear no one ever,
Haya-huasca ampishunga,	*Haya-huasca* will cure you,
Haya-huasca ampishunga.	*Haya-huasca* will cure you.
Sirenapas manchashunga,	The siren too will be afraid of you,
Haya-huasca ampishunga,	*Haya-huasca* will cure you,
Haya-huasca ampishunga.	*Haya-huasca* will cure you.

Nuca runa manchashunga,	The man from the water will be afraid of you,
Haya-huasca ampishunga,	*Haya-huasca* will cure you,
Haya-huasca ampishunga.	*Haya-huasca* will cure you.
Ihanunda mariri,	You will fear no one ever,
Mariri, mariri,	Never, never,
Mariri, mariri.	Never, never.

At the end of this period of seclusion and preparation the novice returns to the world and is immediately recognized as a sorcerer. He goes back to his ordinary occupations, which he pursues during the day; at night he is a sorcerer, his work occult.

The *curanderos* cure with herbs. The *cholos* come to them too and say the results are marvellous.

The *hechiceros* are also called "controllers of hearts". They use plants and bones of animals. The foot of a bird called *shansho* is often used. A woman who wishes to undermine her husband's will, because she has designs on another, goes to a *hechicero* for assistance, taking with her a pair of her husband's pants and of her own knickers (preferably soiled with menstrual blood). These the sorcerer boils for two hours in water which contains *olgarobo* bark. The operation is done in a lonely place. As he stirs the stew with a stick, he repeats over and over to himself: "In the name of *Lucifer*, may the garments of this man and woman cook and may the *olgarobo* change the blood to pure love."

When sufficiently cooled, the clothes are returned to the woman, who gives her husband's pants back to him and puts on her knickers. The husband's will is then enfeebled and she can go with the man she desires.

When one person wants to get another into his power, the *hechiceros* advise the former to administer a potion concocted as follows: powdered cow's horn to be mixed with menstrual blood and dried before a fire, the resulting dry powder being then added to any drink.

Women who find their husbands too domineering are instructed to wrap up his clothes in any stuff that is soiled with menstrual blood.

The *maleros* understand the mysteries of nature and can influence fate. They are sorcerers of an intermediate stage, having not yet reached perfection. They know how to prepare malignant beverages for those they wish to harm, causing 'upheavals'.

Another thing they do is to collect any remains a man may leave after a meal and stuff them into a hole in a *lupuna*, a tree common in the forest, which has, up to ten or twelve feet high, an enormous swollen trunk looking something like a huge demijohn. In doing so they say that the victim will grow fat, as fat as a *lupuna*, and his stomach will burst. Travelling Indians—particularly the porters or *cargueros*—are so frightened of this fate that they scrupulously burn or bury every scrap of refuse when they have meals on the road.

Lastly, there are the *magos*, who are supposed to have reached a state of perfection. They drink infusions of *haya-huasca* which reveals to them many things hidden from the eyes of ordinary people.

On occasions they give the drink to others. The one who drinks it gets drunk and has visions. Quite out of control, he speaks words which the *mago* interprets. For instance, a man who has had a cow stolen will go to a *mago* and be given *haya-huasca*: in his delirium he will see who has stolen it and thus be able next day to go and get it back.

The Lamistas talked to us a lot about birds and animals, some of which were useful for magic purposes.

The *taurilla* is a grey bird with a sad song, frequenting the banks of rivers. One of its bones is useful as a love-charm. It must be killed at five o'clock in the morning, before the hunter has had anything to eat, and buried exactly where it falls. A month later it is carefully dug up and a bone of the right foot taken.

Holding this, a man waylays the girl he loves, taking cover so that she does not see him. As she passes he shuts his left eye and looks at her with the other through the medullary canal of the bone. He goes straight home and shuts himself up for twelve hours during which time no one must see him unless it is the girl in question. She indeed may well come in search of him as she will have immediately fallen in love with him.

Should she not come, at the end of the twelve hours, he goes in search of her.

Finally, the Indians have a belief, which seemed to us of some importance, in a mythical creature, the *chullachaqui*, which means the bandy-legged. His left front leg is shorter than the other, and he appears in the shape of various animals, in solitary places, naturally. The Indian who sees it is exceedingly frightened. He has a look at the creature's left leg and calls it by the name of the animal whose form it has taken. If it then comes towards him, it is certainly a *chullachaqui*. That's the worst omen of all. Something terrible will happen.

XIII

In the Montaña

AT dawn one morning Don Pancho woke us up to say we were moving on into the interior of the country, as had been planned.

"These Indians will drive you crazy if you go on working like that. You never stop. I tried to get hold of you last night, but couldn't find you anywhere. Can you be ready in an hour?"

"Of course."

We dressed quickly and packed up our few belongings, only to wait a long time for the mules which were to take us as far as Tabaloso. The man who was fetching them took so long about it that we thought he'd gone to sleep. At last they came, one by one, and we stuffed our things into the cotton saddle-bags which hung on either side of the saddle.

Don Pancho told us the first stop would be San Miguel on the Rio Mayo and rode off, leading the way. For our part, though used to horses, we found it impossible to coax these beasts along at a normal speed.

The owner of the mules had sent a half-caste along with them, called, somewhat unexpectedly, the *Coronel* (Colonel). He told us we weren't beating the mules hard enough and that we must also use our heels.

When we followed his advice our progress improved. It had been raining all night and the ground was soaked. The rain was now reduced to a fine drizzle. I was afraid of my mule slipping. Had I known these animals better, I wouldn't have worried. They know where to put their feet.

I pressed on and caught Don Pancho up. Reaching the top of a hill a marvellous landscape lay before us. Don Pancho pointed to a village a long way away, straggling up the opposite slope of an immense valley.

"Tabaloso," he said.

That was as far as we were going by mule. From Tabaloso we were to go down the Rio Mayo by *balsa* to its junction with the Huallaga.

"But what about San Miguel?" I asked.

156

"You can't see it. It's tucked away in the bottom of the valley. We've got a long way to go down before we reach it."

For a while, however, the ground was absolutely flat. Vegetation was profuse, the narrow track being in fact a tunnel through the trees.

We met a woman on a mule riding in the opposite direction. After the usual salutations, Don Pancho told her we had been thinking of spending the night at her house in San Miguel.

"I don't know whether I'll be back tonight, Pancho, but that doesn't matter: my José will see to you."

She had some difficulty in brushing past us, so narrow was the path. We had to be careful the big stirrups made of wood and leather didn't get caught.

The path began to go down, gently at first, but soon in giddy zigzags, down thirty or forty yards on one leg, then doubling back on the other, the whole path forming a sort of giant's staircase.

Underfoot, the decomposed rock crumbled at a touch, but at each step the mules seemed to test their foothold before trusting their weight to it. Nor, when we came to steps in the rock twenty inches high, did they make any fuss about them. They jumped down promptly with their forelegs and then gingerly brought their hind legs down after them.

We could thank our stars for having thrown Don Pancho into our path. We couldn't have had a better guide, as everyone told us when they heard we were travelling with him.

"He knows all the ropes and nobody'll dare cheat you."

Now and again we met an Indian. All carried the inevitable *machete*, whose multiple uses we were soon to learn. Some of them carried an oar. We asked Don Pancho why.

He explained they were *balseros*, that is to say *balsa* boatmen. They were returning from a trip down to the Rio Mayo.

"They take a *balsa* downstream and then return on foot."

Towards the end of the descent we took a short cut which was very steep indeed, and we had our work cut out at times to keep our seats. When we reached the valley Don Pancho smiled contentedly.

"We're saved a lot of time by taking the cut."

We crossed an Indian *chacra* full of coffee bushes. The starry flowers shone amongst the leaves and filled the air with scent.

I snatched a red coffee berry as I passed. It wasn't ripe enough to be picked, but it was delicious to eat raw. Hanging from their trees were *chirimoyas*, a succulent creamy-white fruit in a green skin well known in Spain. Unfortunately these were quite unripe. A little further on were bread-fruit trees, and scattered about were banana trees and castor-oil plants.

We reached the bank of the river, and there was San Miguel right opposite us, sleeping in the sunshine. The river ran swiftly. In the middle was an eddy and a patch of foam. We dismounted and waited for someone to come and ferry us across.

"He has to know his job," said Don Pancho. "That whirlpool would capsize anything."

On the other bank all was quiet. The village seemed deserted. Only a few black pigs were nosing around or wallowing in puddles. Some *canoas* were moored up in a little bay, out of the stream. Similar to what we had seen already, they were made from tree-trunks, hollowed out by burning and finished off on the outside with a *machete*.

An Indian appeared and made us a sign. The roar of the water made shouting useless. We understood he was offering to ferry us across and signalled an affirmative.

Casting off the bark-fibre painter, he paddled up into the stream then drifted down to where we were standing.

The three of us got into the *canoa* with the saddles, etc., leaving the *Coronel* with the animals. The crossing was indeed a tricky business, but with the most skilful use of his paddle the Indian got us quickly to the other side.

He then went back for the animals, which crossed one by one, swimming behind the *canoa*, the muleteer holding the bridle.

In the village we found José without difficulty and installed ourselves in his house, where he and his mother kept a little general shop. Everything could be bought in it—everything, that is, which was regarded as necessary according to their very simple standards.

The rest of the day slipped quickly past. A *siesta*. A bathe. Many went down for a dip in the river, some prompted by pleasure, others by cleanliness. One of us chose a spot where he was screened by a large tree which hung out over the river. A little further down, men and women were bathing together, married couples, no doubt, for the Indians are very particular in matters of decency, and all bathing is done naked. The women had come to a little creek there, carrying their children and accompanied by their husbands. Undressing, they began washing, starting with their long hair which they lathered thoroughly, then dipping their amber-coloured bodies in the water.

The women kept to the banks. The men, on the other hand, after a thorough wash in the shallows, struck out into the stream. One even braved the whirlpool, in which he totally disappeared for a while. The stream carried him out of it, however, and swept him over to the other bank.

Most of the women were young and beautifully made. Neither too slim, nor too plump, their torsos were attached to their hips with a miraculous elasticity, and their long straight legs were gracefully curved at calf and buttock.

When our indiscreet onlooker emerged, he wondered whether the Indians wouldn't be angry at having been surprised at such a moment, but no. Though they had seen him well enough, they merely donned a piece of clothing and began to wash their little ones.

A tiny girl, too young to walk, crawled down towards the water. Her mother tried to stop her but in vain. Then the father intervened, picked the child up and, swimming with one arm, took it right out into the swiftly moving water. That should have taught it a lesson; but no, a few minutes later it was making fearlessly for the river again.

In the village was a house in which a child had just died. The mother's lamentations floated out into the twilight and continued all through the night. Her husband laughed, saying he didn't care, since he was not the father of it. The real father kept out of sight. And the mother went on howling, at times drowning our conversation.

We went into the house. The little girl had been laid out on a table, with a cross and a few flowers. Through the cotton stuff which covered the body, which, in the heat, was already beginning to decompose, we could see a greatly swollen stomach, and guessed she had died of one of the abdominal diseases so common in hot climates. Brothers and sisters played heedlessly round the bier.

Next day we were off early for Tabaloso, named after a Spanish marquess who had been a governor of the region in the 17th century.

The track this time was less hilly. It led through a forest of enormous trees and a tangle of lianas which tried to cling to our stirrups. It was slow going, partly because our mules were tired by the previous day's ride. Sometimes we came to recent clearings in which the tree stumps were still smouldering.

Before reaching Tabaloso, the track led down to a wide stretch of grassland which looked as though it would be good pasture. Much of the land was cut up into enclosed fields, and there were many gates to open and shut, some of which, stiff and heavy, were quite troublesome.

Our mules were on their last legs. At each settlement they tried to make for the huts, and it was all we could do to bring them back onto the track.

In sight of our destination, the track began to climb again, passing enormous black rocks which absorbed the rays of the sun. The climate had changed since we left Lamas, becoming much hotter, though not sufficiently to trouble us seriously.

Entering Tabaloso we were the focus of all eyes, the people here being unused to visitors. Men and women ran into the street to gaze at us, and in no time it was known all over the town that two *gringos* (foreigners) had arrived with Don Pancho.

We put up at the house of Don Pancho's brother-in-law, where we had the good fortune to meet an Indian schoolmaster, who was eager to help us with our linguistic studies. For two whole days without stopping we were writing down Quechua words in phonetic script. It was a race against time, for we knew we should have to move on as soon as Don Pancho had bought and collected his bales of cotton and sacks of coffee.

The schoolmaster, Rodolfo Chuyutalli Chavez, was a typical Indian in spite of being not quite a pure one, his mother having had a dash of *cholo* blood. What was remarkable was that his schoolmaster's culture had done nothing to weaken his interest in that of his own race.

We had hesitated before undertaking this work. Quechua is a language sufficiently known for there to be grammars and dictionaries in existence—but always dealing with Cuzco Quechua. What we heard around us was so different that we thought it worth while recording. An old Indian had said to us:

"This isn't the same Quechua at all. When I did my military service in the Sierras I couldn't understand a word of what anybody said."

"When I was a student in Lima," added Chavez, "I ran into many who knew the Quechua of the Sierras. Listening to them I found that many words were recognizably similar, different though they were. On the other hand I'm sure there are many words here which they haven't got at all."

We were at it up to the last minute when Don Pancho came to drag us away. Once again we mounted our mules, which had been resting in the fields.

We did not ride alone. A small caravan of Indian porters, *cargueros*,

Tabaloso

Indian girl fetch-
ing water

carrying Don Pancho's merchandise, came with us on that two-hour journey to the Rio Mayo. We already knew of them by reputation. They are the most doughty porters in the world, as they were to prove to us that day. The sacks of coffee were heavy enough at 176 lb., but some of the bales of cotton weighed a couple of hundredweight and more, the heaviest being 264 lb.

The *carguero's* load is carried on his back, though the weight is largely taken by the head. A circular band of cotton webbing

Carguero

called *pretina*, an inch and a half in width, runs over the head and under the bottom of the load, which, thus secured, can be carried for hours at a stretch. *Llevar a lomo de indeginas*, to carry by native back. That is the phrase used, and it is not a very flattering one either, since *lomo* is the word for the back of an animal.

All goods coming from Lamas and Tarapoto are transported—and very economically—by this means. Sometimes missionaries too. For them a *cajon* is used, a sort of packing-case rigged up as a chair, but the method of carriage is the same, the weight being taken on the head by means of a *pretina*. A more luxurious method used by

L

some missionaries is a hammock carried as a litter by two or more men, but for the most part those who are strong enough prefer to travel on their own two feet or by mule.

At the Rio Mayo the *cargueros* came in one by one, and Don Pancho, waiting for them, weighed each load on arrival.

The strength of their backs is a great asset to the Lamistas, many of whom earn their livelihood in this way. When we marvelled at what we had seen, Don Pancho pooh-poohed it.

"That's nothing," he said. "Six miles! Child's play! They often do three or four times that in a day, and repeat it three or four days in succession."

The method of payment of *cargueros* is very variable. Some get five *soles* a day, which is about half a crown. Often they are paid in kind, with a couple of pounds of dried fish, for instance, or, more rarely, a length of stuff, which they sell during the journey as opportunity offers.

The tariff is indeed so low that goods can often be sold at the same price as they are in the place they came from, three days' journey away.

While Don Pancho was dealing with the *cargueros* we sat by the Rio Mayo, where a woman, Francesca, was searching for nits in a little girl's head. Francesca, who was not quite all there, was to be our travelling companion down the river.

Five *balsas* were to carry the cargo and passengers. Don Pancho was a bit jumpy about the business. *Balsas* often capsized, he told us, in which case all the cargo was lost.

"You'd better go and have a look at the *balsas*," he said. "They're finishing them off now."

We found them in the shelter of a little creek. They were quite different craft altogether from the *balsas* we have described on Lake Titicaca. These were rafts made of very light tree-trunks lashed together with lianas. The big ends of the trunks were all forward, so that the after ends were slightly splayed.

About twenty inches above them a platform of *palma brava* was designed to keep the cargo clear of the water. It could also take passengers. When a raft was exclusively for passengers, a more elaborate superstructure was erected, with a roof to protect them from the sun, which beats down mercilessly on these enormous rivers.

XIV

By *Balsa* Down the Mayo

LOADING the *balsas* took a long time, for everything had to be securely lashed, but at last it was finished. Our mules had already departed, swimming the river again, as they had before at San Miguel.

We were fascinated by the rafts, which seemed to promise excitement. We thought of the whirlpool at San Miguel and wondered how these fragile things would stand such buffeting. And Don Pancho hadn't stopped grumbling about the rapids all day.

He told us to choose bales of cotton to sit on, and we clambered on board. The crew of the raft consisted of three *balseros*, dressed only in shorts, equipped with long oars which, however, were not really for rowing but for steering and manœuvring.

They cast off, and, using their oars with great vigour, they paddled us out into the stream. They never stopped shouting. The middle one of the three, who were all forward, gave orders to the other two. When they were not too preoccupied with the raft, they argued or chaffed the simple-minded Francesca, who was now enthroned on a bale of cotton.

"Look out," urged Don Pancho. "Here's the first rapid. Hold tight."

One of the *balseros* implored the *rio*:

"Do not be angry. Let not these rapids drown us, nor those which follow."

The smooth surface of the water was suddenly broken, being thrown up into a seething mass of bubbles, the crest of which was three feet above the river level. We all hung on, the *balseros* with their feet, while they worked their oars like mad to steer us clear of the rocks, shouting more wildly than ever to keep their courage up.

The tree-trunks heaved and strained at their lashings. At times they and our stalwart *balseros* practically disappeared in the foam and spray. It seemed impossible that our raft would hold together.

It did. The cords of liana and bark-fibre, more elastic than any European rope, gave—and held. These lashings could in fact stand up to anything except being cut by rocks, some of which were sharp as knives. Naturally, if that happened, the raft broke up at once, scattering cargo and passengers on the flood.

More than once we bumped a rock in the shallows, but no harm was done.

This, of course, was just the sort of thing we had come for, and we enjoyed every moment of it, to the surprise of the others.

"These *gringos* don't seem to be afraid," they muttered among themselves.

"Shall we come to any bigger ones?" we asked.

"You wait! That was nothing!"

We grinned and our prestige soared to fresh heights.

The interminable windings of the Mayo reminded us of the Beni and the Mamore. Here too we encountered tree-trunks stuck into the muddy bottom, as dangerous for our raft as they had been for the boats on the Beni.

The heat was terrific, but we didn't complain. We were getting used to this climate and learning to like it. As one of us said:

"I always feel happy when I see a banana tree, as I know I'm going to like the climate."

We looked forward impatiently to the next rapids. There were plenty to come. Except for the feeble-minded Francesca, who giggled innocently, we were the only ones to think them fun. The others knew too much.

At San Miguel we stopped for a moment, and a certain Oscar, one of Don Pancho's men, whom we had hardly seen so far, told us we were to shift to his *balsa*. I just had time for a dip in the river during the change-over. Then we started downstream again.

"But where's Francesca?" we asked.

"She's staying the night at San Miguel," said Oscar, "and coming down in the last *balsa*. Don Pancho's orders."

Oscar turned out to be a pleasant travelling companion. A boy of eighteen, he had been with Don Pancho two years already, and was attached to him.

"And where are we going to spend the night?"

"At Maceda. At the last moment Don Pancho thought you'd better not stop at San Miguel. He meant to tell you himself, but he had to go off to find a man who'd promised him some coffee. He'll catch us up tomorrow, early in the afternoon."

Reaching Maceda, on the left bank of the Mayo, our *balseros* said to us:

"We're tired. You ought to stand us a *chuchuwasha*."

"What's that?"

"It's a tree; and a drink made with the bark soaked in *aguardiente*."

"What's it do to you?"

It strengthened bones, we learnt, and was good for the nerves. It also cured rheumatism and asthma. Lastly it was an aphrodisiac. Many of them drank it, however, just because they liked it.

We entered the first shop we could find and ordered *chuchuwasha*. They brought us a flagon of the stuff, which was mixed with the traditional *trago*. The *trago* or tot is a glass of *aguardiente*, which goes the round from mouth to mouth regardless of any rules of hygiene. Naturally we took our places in the round and tasted the *chuchuwasha*.

"It's like nothing on earth—but it's good all the same."

That was our verdict. The time passed quickly; it was getting dark. We just managed to look round the place in the last flicker of daylight. Much like San Miguel or Tabaloso. When we got back to our quarters night had fallen. After a rapid meal we turned in.

As half the population were half-castes, we didn't expect to come across anything particularly interesting at Maceda. We were mistaken.

Jean-Luc went out early next morning with his camera, while Oscar and I wandered about in search of a hand-loom. We ran into each other at the weaver's. He showed us his loom, a horizontal one. Unfortunately it was too dark in the place to take a photograph.

"Can we see it working?"

"No. You can't weave in the morning."

"Why not?"

"The warp keeps breaking. You need sun for weaving, lots of sun."

"Can't one weave at night?"

"Quite impossible."

We were interested, as we always were in the customs surrounding trades. The Dogons of the Sudan only weave in daylight, for "weaving is speaking, and speech is light"!

On closer questioning, we gathered that it was the dampness of the river which underlay this custom. The cotton absorbs moisture during the night, and it is only after the sun has been up for some hours that it is again dry enough to be worked. But we strongly suspected there was a bit of magic in it too.

Jean-Luc went off again, looking for material for film and snapshot. It was getting hot and Oscar and I went back to our hut and lay down. A not particularly pretty half-caste girl came in and sat down in a corner.

For a while she chatted of this and that. Then turning to me, she said:

"I've never seen such good-looking *gringos* as you two. What's your name?"

"Bernardo."

"And the other one?"

"Juan-Lucas."

"You know, Oscar, they're really beautiful *gringos*, dark, and with hair on their chests."

Oscar and I smiled and answered playfully, but the *cholo* girl continued:

"*Gringos* are generally so ugly. Fair. It's ugly to be fair. But these two! I'd like them to give me a baby."

"But you can't have a baby by two men at the same time," answered Oscar, laughing.

"One this year. The other can come back next. I'm not the only one. All the other girls would like it too."

Amusing as the proposition was, it was somewhat alarming. And it was not without difficulty that the claimant was got rid of.

We were still on the look-out for sorcerers. Not too easy to come by, as the Indians kept that side of their lives out of sight. And, when we did find one, he generally laughed, and shut up like a clam, or pretended he wasn't one.

Walking through the town, we came upon a group of people who were building a house. Oscar, who knew them all, pointed to one.

"There. That's a sorcerer."

He was a young man with a dazed expression on his face. We decided to wait for the builders to finish their work.

"When you've done," we said, "come and have a *trago* with us."

They accepted. Meanwhile, they made us taste some *masato* and *chicha* they had with them. The former is a drink made of *yuca*, the Peruvian name for manioc. *Chicha*, on the other hand, is made with maize, and it is essential to the process that part of the maize flour should be thoroughly masticated by "a boy with a clean mouth". The result, anyhow, is a refreshing drink with a pleasant taste, reputedly very nourishing.

"There we are! We've finished now," said the workmen.

"Let's go then."

The sorcerer knew no Spanish, so we got hold of a *cholo* girl to act as interpreter. As a matter of fact she answered most of our questions off her own bat, only referring to him in cases of doubt.

The conversation turned once again on *chuchuwasha*.

"Aren't there any other uses?" we asked, having told them what we knew.

"Yes, as a poultice."

"How is it made?"

"The powdered bark is boiled for five or six hours to a thick paste."

"Put on hot?"

"Lukewarm."

Used for testicle troubles. A decoction made from *chuchuwasha* root and *olgarobo* bark is used for bone fractures, being taken internally twice daily.

Our interpreter, Rosalia, frequently employed the Spanish words *con dieta*, which combine the meanings of regimen and cure, though, as regards regimen, it often refers specifically to what must be avoided rather than what must be eaten. The butter *con dieta*, for instance, which she described to us after consulting the sorcerer, consists in going without butter for a month, eating onions, beans, and *aji*. This last looks and tastes somewhat like red peppers, though much stronger. During the *con dieta*, cold baths must be taken and strong drink avoided.

The *con dieta* for women involves abstaining from sexual intercourse for six months. With the taking (under supervision) of *hayahuasca* it forms part of the initiation of a sorcerer, but it is also used for the treatment of rheumatism and as a general tonic. In this latter case sexual intercourse is abstained from for three months, the sap of a plant called *hoje* is taken for a week, and the patient must neither eat salt nor bathe. Two weeks of bathing in sun-warmed water follows, then a month's bathing in cold.

A bathing treatment on somewhat similar lines is recommended to prevent swelling.

Rosalia was a mine of information on all subjects and, while waiting for Don Pancho, we plied her with questions. It was from her that we learnt, for instance, that the teasing of raw cotton was done by hand, no carding instrument being used. After the seed was removed, the fibres were separated by the fingers one by one. The spinning was done just as Candelaria Sangama had demonstrated.

When the builders left us we wandered about with Rosalia. There were Indian women in the streets with pitchers on their heads which they had filled from the river.

"What do they use to dye their skirts that blue, Rosalia?"

"A plant."

She pointed to some bushes growing by some Indian houses.

"What's it called?"

"I don't know. The Indians won't tell."

We picked one of the pale green leaves which, pressed between the leaves of a book, at once turned a dark Prussian blue.

Here too, the Indians, men and women alike, wore iguana bracelets and anklets. According to Rosalia that was why they had such well-shaped arms and legs. Graceful they certainly were, but I couldn't refrain from expressing a doubt of its being due to the properties of iguana skin.

She was giving us some further medical prescriptions when Oscar came to fetch us. Lunch was ready. During the meal Don Pancho turned up.

"I've had to leave Francesca at San Miguel," he said. "She spent the night making nine *balseros* happy. She can do as she likes, but I'm not going to have my *balsas* turned into brothels."

Laughing over Francesca's misbehaviour, we finished eating, then went down to the river. Oscar was told to go ahead with the *balsa* he had taken yesterday, while we went on Don Pancho's. There were two passengers on it already, a toothless old *cholo* and her niece. Before long, Don Pancho said:

"We'll soon be coming to the worst rapids of all. Don't talk to the *balseros* any more. They need to keep their minds on their work, or they'll be doing something stupid."

The *balseros* were for the moment quite unconcerned, laughing and chattering. They kept jumping into the calm water, leaving the raft to drift downstream unaided, then clambering out, naked, their fringes plastered down on their foreheads. When another *balsa* drew close to ours the youngest swam over to it and returned with some booty—a bottle of *aguardiente* and three *inguires* (green bananas). They didn't fail to offer us a *trago*, and we drank the health of the crew it had been stolen from.

Suddenly the fun ceased, laughter died down. Our three *balseros* now sat gloomily on the forward part of the raft, hardly exchanging a word. They glanced at the *gringos*, perhaps expecting a joke, but we did as we were told and kept our mouths shut. Not from choice however: we were still sceptical of the danger, and went on filling out notes we had jotted down at Maceda and filming the river banks and the *balsas* coming down behind us.

Don Pancho, of course, was thinking of his cotton and his coffee. We heard him say to the old woman:

"These *gringos* are fools. They don't realize the danger."

Then, turning to us, he went on:

"You'd better stow away everything you can—your cameras, your notebooks—unless you don't mind losing them. And stop moving about, or you may be washed away yourselves."

"Can't I take a film of the rapids?" asked Jean-Luc.

"All right—as long as you hold on. I'll pass you up some *sogas*."

He passed up the ends of some liana lashings that were secured to the tree-trunks.

"And wedge yourself in between two bales of cotton. Seriously, these rapids are no joke."

Unable to hold on to the *sogas* and his film-camera, Jean-Luc appealed to me.

"You hold on to them with one hand and grip my foot with the other."

The others caught hold of *sogas* too. A dull roar ahead told us Don Pancho was not being unduly fussy. The *rio* narrowed and, whipped up into foam, passed between two threatening rocks. The *rio* at this point was a veritable waterchute of quite extraordinary violence, as can be gathered from the fact that the river level fell fully six feet in a very short distance.

The raft pitched and strained, the tree-trunks screeched as they rubbed together. One corner of the *balsa* bumped violently into the right-hand rock as the force of the stream caught us. For several seconds tree-trunks and *balseros* were lost to view. And then we shipped it green, right over platform, cargo, passengers and all.

Emerging from that ordeal, the same thing happened again, and then a third time. Finally we shot out into calmer water and the other *balsas* followed.

No. Don Pancho hadn't exaggerated.

One *balsa* drifted ahead of us and was soon out of sight. After two or three bends in the river we caught up with it again, to find it turning helplessly round and round in a whirlpool from which no efforts of the *balseros* could extricate it. The whirlpool seemed simply to be making fun of them. We passed and left them behind. That evening when they rejoined us at our stopping-place the *balseros* told us they had had a long struggle to get the raft free.

Another danger spot was where several tree-trunks had got stuck in the bottom, the water swirling past them. As there was little space between them, it required good steering to get through, made all the more difficult by the fact that our little fleet arrived all in a bunch. One raft, that had made for the right-hand gap, scraped the river bank and was lucky to escape being wrecked. The after-part, swinging out into the stream, got caught by a stump on its port quarter. Again it was lucky, however; it managed to swing clear.

At about six in the evening, we heard a loud noise in the forest which flanked the river. It sounded something like the roar of a powerful ventilator.

"What's that?"

"It's a bird. And when you hear it, you don't need to look at your watch. You know it's six o'clock and will soon be dark."

It was the *cacapana*. And the *balseros* cried in chorus:

"There! The *cacapana* has sung," meaning it was time to stop.

A hut appeared on the right bank, and they immediately steered their craft towards it and beached them.

We spent the night there. Next morning we arrived at the junction of the Mayo with the Huallaga. There we had to take leave of the *balsas*, which were proceeding down the Huallaga river as far as Yurimaguas.

As we were getting our gear ashore, we saw a *balsa* floating downstream with neither cargo nor *balseros*.

"What's it doing, drifting all on its own?" we asked.

"It's come to the end of its trip and been abandoned, being of no further use. It'll sink sooner or later."

"But why should it be of no further use? It could take a cargo down to Yurimaguas, for instance?"

"It's not done. Wood's plentiful, and the *balseros* prefer to construct a new raft for every trip. Partly superstition, perhaps, but it's not altogether unreasonable. You've seen the strains these craft are subjected to. The lashings would soon chafe through. Indeed I wouldn't have anything to do with *balsas* if there was any alternative. I'm always relieved when a trip's over. They're wrecked often enough and you must always allow for losses in counting your costs."

It was indeed an almost inescapable means of transport. Tinned food, for instance, or beer, which had to come from Lima to Tarapoto, would go by lorry to Tingo Maria, thence by *balsa* down the Huallaga to Yurimaguas, the final lap being done 'by native back', *a lomo de indigenas*. So frequent were disasters that it was sometimes cheaper to send goods air freight. When transporting petrol, on the other hand, the risk was negligible. The drums floated and could be recovered.

On account of risks in transport, shopkeepers at Tarapoto preferred to pay only for such goods as were safely delivered, but it wasn't every wholesaler who was prepared to trade on those terms, in which case they had to adjust their prices to cover losses.

Needless to say, no insurance company was willing to enter this field.

The other *balsas* arrived one by one. With Oscar and Don Pancho, who had regained his serenity, we went to have a late lunch, for it was four o'clock in the afternoon.

Taking our coffee by the Rio Mayo, we got our notebooks and again began firing off questions, returning once more to the subject of childbirth.

"When a woman feels the pains coming on, some matrons come to help her, and give her *malva* (mallow) tea."

"If delivery is delayed," I said, consulting my notebook, "the matrons wash the husband and beat the woman with the clothes the husband has taken off."

"And do you know," added Oscar, "that, if this doesn't work, they hang her up by her hands from the ceiling?"

"No, I didn't, though I knew nomad Arabs did."

"Is the newborn baby washed?"

"Yes. And the mother too with a decoction of *chuchuwasha* and other herbs."

"And she's given *aguardiente* and *chuchuwasha* to drink. That's to stop bleeding."

"And the afterbirth?"

"The matrons throw it away in a ravine."

"Does the mother get up at once?"

"No," answered Don Pancho. "Not for a week. At the end of that, she's thoroughly washed and can go back to her ordinary life."

We were interrupted by the *balseros*, who had all been eating together. They came to say good-bye. Don Pancho was not going with them any further. He gave them final instructions and they floated off, waving to us from the distance.

"Do you intend to trace the life of an Indian from the cradle to the grave?" asked Don Pancho as we settled down again.

"Exactly," we answered, laughing. "And with all his customs, rites, and superstitions. All his medicines too."

"Then you'll still be here two years from now."

"Ten, perhaps! So much the better. So far we've only made a start and are counting on coming back again."

We were waiting for a *gondola* to take us back to Tarapoto. There we would be bidding farewell to Don Pancho and Oscar and going on to Lamas the following day.

Till it arrived, we talked of baptisms, of which there were many sorts, and of the many different sorts of godparents whose office was not always concerned with baptism. At Jesus de Machaca, for instance, we had heard of a *compadre* (godfather) of *lutoca-kacharina*, *lutoca* meaning a period of mourning and *kacharina* the termination of it (with a *fiesta*).

As soon as the *gondola* appeared, Don Pancho cut short our conversation and hurried us off. An hour and a half later we were in Tarapoto, where our first concern was to book two seats in next day's *gondola* for Lamas. Then we had dinner with Oscar, Don Pancho having gone straight home, where he knew his wife would be waiting for him.

In our hotel that night we were going through our material, sorting and filing, when Jean-Luc suddenly felt unwell, being assailed by the troubles which had already bothered him in Bolivia.

Afraid of his being taken seriously ill in that country, we made a hurried decision: he would return immediately to France, while I went on with the work so long as finances held out.

We packed our bags, dividing up objects of common property after considering who could make best use of them. Jean-Luc was taking a plane which left at the same time as my *gondola*, so I was unable to accompany my partner to the airport.

Our farewells were multilingual: "*Good luck! Buena suerte! Nach Paris! Hacia Lamas!*"

And then together in our own tongue: "*Bon voyage!*"

The truck with Jean-Luc in it drove off towards the airport, disappearing in a cloud of yellow dust, leaving me reproaching myself for not having looked after my friend's health better, and gloomily brooding over the loss of the most perfect travelling companion.

XV

The Lamista Wedding

HARDLY had I lost sight of Jean-Luc when I ran into Don Pancho on the main square.

"Ah! I was looking for you. Your *gondola's* broken down and won't go till tomorrow."

"All right. Tomorrow it must be. Thanks for telling me."

On my way back to the hotel, however, I made up my mind to travel that day if any sort of vehicle was going. I asked several people.

"Is there any car or lorry going to Lamas today?"

"Not now. There was one, but it left first thing this morning."

In the hotel two men were sitting at a little table drinking beer. I sat down and ordered a lemon *pisco*.

"The petrol's come," said one of the men.

"Can you let me have a drop for my electric generator?" asked the innkeeper.

"I'm afraid I can't. I've got to be off to Lamas in a minute. All the drums are sealed up."

I butted in promptly.

"You're going to Lamas?"

"Yes."

"Can you take me?"

"By all means."

"When?"

"Now."

And in a minute or two I was perched up on the drums, which in the heat gave off a heady vapour. I raised my head as high as I could to breathe, but it was no good: I couldn't escape the fumes. When we arrived at Lamas after a good two hours' drive I was half way to being overcome.

I was dropped outside my former quarters and immediately went to have a bathe, hoping it would clear my head. It didn't do much good. I was determined to waste no time, however, so I went to look up our friends Guillermo and Arquimedes at the school inspector's office.

"Hallo. You again? But what have you done to Juan-Lucas?"

"Shipped him back home."

I explained what had happened.

"Well, well! We never expected to see you again. . . . But you've been cleaning your clothes with benzine."

I explained what had happened to me.

". . . I've got a headache and I feel sick."

"Say no more about it. We'll put that right in a moment. We'll give you something you don't know about, a *trago* of *aguardiente* and *chuchuwasha*."

"You can't teach me much about *chuchuwasha*," I answered. "I've been living with *balseros* on the Rio Mayo."

"Dear, dear!" said Guillermo ruefully. "He knows everything, this chap! . . . But really it's wonderful stuff. Come along."

They dragged me round to the Social Club and the *chuchuwasha* did all that was claimed of it. I was myself again in no time.

Guillermo soon left us, as he had to go home.

"Now look here, Arquimedes," I said when he had gone, "I don't know quite everything yet, and I'm going to start asking questions here and now."

"Yes, of course," he answered thoughtfully.

I could see there was something at the back of his mind, and the next moment he asked:

"Are you a good walker?"

"Any distance you like. Why?"

"There's a wedding on at a village some distance away. I'm going this afternoon, as I'm acting as godfather. It means walking several hours. If it hadn't been for the petrol fumes making you ill, I'd have asked you to come along."

"When do you start?"

"At two."

"I'll come."

"If you really feel fit enough. . . . It'll certainly be worth seeing."

At the stated time I picked Arquimedes up outside the office. We started at once. Leaving the main square, we went down one side of the church and entered a long straight street, baked by the sun and absolutely deserted at that hour of the day, when everyone else was having his *siesta*.

"What's it called, this village we're going to?"

"Pacchilla."

"Are there many Indians there?"

"They're all Indians."

Arquimedes told me he had often played the part of *compadre* at a wedding. In this one, the bride was his wife's godchild. His wife would be there too, of course. She had left for Pacchilla in the morning with the party of Indians.

At the outskirts of Lamas our street became a narrow track flanked by young bushes. It struck off to the north-east, soon plunging into a forest of half-grown trees such as is often seen in the neighbourhood of a village. Walking hard and speaking little we went down into a valley at the bottom of which ran a stream, almost dry at this season. Passing a *carguero* we gave him the conventional greeting: "*Ola.*"

At the bottom, Arquimedes said:

"We began at four o'clock this morning. We had forty Indians in the house. At six we went to the church and the priest performed the marriage service."

"And then they all went back to their village, did they?"

"Yes. Of course things are done differently when people of the town get married. They go back from the church to their particular quarter and the *funcia* begins at once. In this case, Pacchilla being so far, it's put off till the next day."

"*Funcia?*"

"Yes, *funcia*. That's our word for the wedding *fiesta*. But you don't know much about Lamista weddings, do you?"

"Assume I know nothing at all. Fire away."

Slackening his pace, Arquimedes began:

"As soon as an Indian can carry a hundredweight on his back, he begins to think about founding a family. He looks around for a girl he'd like to marry.

"He buys a cyclamen-coloured handkerchief and a comb studded with bright stones and chased with silver. Then he hangs about in places where the object of his choice is likely to pass. Taking her by surprise, he tries to thrust the comb wrapped in the handkerchief into her blouse. If he does, the marriage is arranged."

"Supposing the girl isn't willing?"

"She tries to stop him. In any case she puts up a bit of a struggle— it's the proper thing to do—but if she likes him she puts up merely a formal one."

"She might really want to stop him and still not succeed."

"Then there's nothing more she can do about it."

"And if she does succeed, is she safe?"

"For the time being."

"Has she had any previous warning that the young man's after her?"

"Oh yes, for he plays a plaintive serenade in the evenings outside her house."

"On what?"

"On a pipe. Something like the *kéna* you heard at Tiahuanaco, only shorter. At least that's the traditional instrument. The mouth-organ's taking its place more and more. And of course, when he plays, her parents know too."

"Can he catch the girl anywhere?"

"She must be alone. Often it's done when she goes for water. Often the water of a stream is run off along a conduit of hollowed-out tree-trunks, so that, at the end, it falls from a height. That saves the women having to stoop. Useful for shower-baths too. Such places are often tucked away in the trees; when she returns, the girl may have to climb up a slippery bank, stepping from stone to stone. She carries her pitcher full of water on her head, cushioned by a grummet. You can imagine she's rather at a disadvantage if he suddenly jumps out of the bushes.

"Even so, it's not as easy as you might think. Our girls are strongly built, and she has a good chance of resisting if she really wants to. Otherwise, as I said, it's all over. From that moment they're engaged. When she gets home, the girl hands the comb over to her parents; they know they must get ready to receive the young man and his parents, who will soon be paying a formal call to claim the girl's hand.

"A mutual friend comes round to announce the impending visit, which takes place between midnight and three in the morning. The visitors may if they like bring a friend or two with them. They bring a pig and a few hens, as well as something to drink, *chicha*, *masato*, and *aguardiente*.

"They are received by the girl's father. The mother keeps out of sight, though she takes good care to see what goes on.

"At first nothing is said of the object of the visit. Only when the presents have been given and a calabash of *aguardiente* has gone the round does the young man's father say solemnly: 'Before any speak ill of my son and your daughter, I have to ask the hand of your daughter, so that they may marry and no evil things be said.'

"To this, the girl's father answers neither yes nor no. And at this moment her mother appears, to offer another round of *aguardiente*.

By Balsa down the Rio Maya

Maceda

Jean-Luc Javal on the Rio Maya

"Only then does the father consent, though conditionally. The young man must prove his worth. He must carry a load of four *arrobas* from one place to another, from Lamas, for instance, to Mayabamba, an *arroba* being two stone. In other words he must carry a hundredweight for five days' march."

"Why should the girl's father want to test his strength?"

"To test his earning capacity. And you know, it's nothing much, a hundredweight—not for a Lamista. You've seen the loads they carry."

"Indeed I've seen them carry more than twice that amount. But tell me: subject to that condition, is the father bound to consent?"

"Not absolutely. But if he refuses it means a blood feud between the two families and sooner or later someone will be killed. That's extremely rare."

"And if the young man can't carry the stipulated load?"

"That's very rare too. For one thing, a chap that couldn't would hardly think of marrying. And then—you've been studying native medicine: you've probably heard of *sanango*. . . ."

"Yes. It's a stimulant and a tonic. It's used as a cure for rheumatism, old age, and debility."

"Just so. For any sort of weakness. And a young man who can't do the trick without it takes *sanango* in *aguardiente*. Then he can."

We were now some distance from Lamas and much lower down. Its church tower was masked by intervening hills.

But the path led upwards again and we were soon at the top of a small hill. I asked Arquimedes to stop for a moment to look at the landscape. Here and there were *ceticos*, moderate-sized bushes with a white stem, used for making paper. At the edge of our track were coffee bushes, whose starry white flowers scented the air. They had sprung up, presumably, from berries dropped in transport.

We went on, down the other side of the hill till we reached a little river, which we had to ford. While crossing, I slipped on a wet stone, but picked myself up, laughing. This little mishap was to stand me in good stead later on.

After three hours' walking, Arquimedes told me we were half way.

And he had been keeping up quite a good pace in spite of talking. Arquimedes began again:

"As soon as consent has been given, the young people's parents put their heads together to fix the date of the wedding and work out the quantity of food and drink that will be required.

M

"Then the *padrinos* (godfathers) are chosen. Very often they like to have a half-caste, or *tinterillo*, who has pull with the authorities and who will then be able, if difficulties arise, to smooth the young couple's path.

"Next, one of the *padrinos* is chosen to go with the couple to see the priest and make arrangements for the religious ceremony. The priest asks a number of questions to make sure there is no impediment. Then he gets the couple to put their thumbprints on the indenture of betrothal, for of course neither of them can sign their names. From that moment they are officially engaged.

"On their wedding day they present themselves at about five in the morning at the *padrino's*—as they did at my place this morning. My wife and I dressed them up for the church—the bride in a black skirt, white blouse, and a black silk veil which allowed only her face to be seen. The bridegroom's clothes are less important—shirt and trousers of any colour he likes, and a *ʒarita* (straw hat).

"After the service they go back to the *padrino's* to change. If they're in their own village they get straight into their *fiesta* clothes—you'll be seeing them tomorrow—but if, as in this case, they live far away, they put their everyday clothes on again.

"And that's about all I need tell you. The *funcia* you'll see for yourself. But don't forget I'm there to help you understand it all. If there's anything you want to know, don't hesitate to ask."

"You're quite right, Arquimedes. If you tell me too much now, it'll take the edge off it."

We walked on through the forest. The track seemed endless. Night was falling, but we had not yet reached Pacchilla. Fire-flies darted about in the twilight. Arquimedes caught one, maintaining it was just as much use as an electric torch. The country was changing, the ups and downs being longer now than over the little hills we had been crossing.

"We're nearly there."

A plateau. The track turned slightly to the left, and a moment later Arquimedes gave the welcome news:

"Here we are."

It was quite dark now—had been for some time. My one wish was to go to bed, but the Lamistas take hospitality seriously and I had first to get through a much too copious meal.

In the dark I was unable to get my bearings or even to form an idea of the size of the village. In the room where we sat, the light of a single candle just enabled me to make out the walls of *palma brava* and the few pieces of furniture with which I had already been made familiar at Candelaria Sangama's and in the various other houses I had visited.

"Eat," said Arquimedes.

"But I'm not hungry any more. And I'm so sleepy I could drop."

His wife came up to me. I had seen her once in Lamas and introduced myself.

"I could tell it was you by your beard," she answered. "Our men don't have them."

I had let mine grow during our travels, to save the trouble of shaving.

"Eat," said Arquimedes, "or they may be offended."

Two children came in, a boy of ten and a little girl of five.

"My children," said Arquimedes.

The last mouthful swallowed, we said good night.

"You're coming with me to my house," said my friend.

"Your house? I didn't know you had a house here."

"I haven't exactly—not one of my own. But custom demands that the *padrino* has a house. He mustn't stay with either the bride's family or the bridegroom's. So somebody had to lend me one. At Lamas it would have been different: the things that have to be done at the *padrino's* house would have been done at home."

"How did your wife get here? Did she have to walk?"

"No, she came by mule, with the little one behind her. The boy came on foot."

The 'padrino's house' was smaller than the one we had left but was otherwise exactly like it.

"Legs aching?" asked Arquimedes.

"No. But that walk's made me sleepy. There's nothing like a walk as a soporific."

.   .   .   .   .

Pacchilla. Dawn.

I woke up slowly. My bamboo mattress was hard. Daylight was beginning to filter through the lattice walls. I turned over onto my side. Through the chinks I could see Indians passing and a few children playing nearby.

"What's the time?"

No answer. Arquimedes was already up, and had crept out without disturbing me. He was no doubt going about his *padrino* business.

I got up. From the daylight I judged it to be about six. Like an Indian or an old French peasant, I was becoming used to telling the time by the sun.

Arquimedes went by and I called him.

"Where can I have a wash?"

"Here's someone who'll take you to the spring."

My guide spoke a little Spanish. He told me to come with him.

"*Vente conmigo.*"

At the spring several Indians, stark naked, were washing industriously under the water that poured from a hollowed-out tree-trunk. My presence caused them no embarrassment. I followed their example, and the cold water woke me up thoroughly and effaced any stiffness due to the long trek or the hard bed. My guide waited for me, chatting in Quechua with the others.

Suddenly one of them rapped out something in Quechua and the men hurriedly put on their pants, I following suit. A woman appeared, in a leisurely way filled her *cantaro*, then turned back towards the village, when the washing was resumed.

When I found Arquimedes again, he looked down at my feet.

"Why don't you put your shoes on?"

"They got properly soaked yesterday when I slipped into the river and they're not dry yet. It doesn't matter: I'm quite all right like this."

I told him what had happened at the spring.

"Oh yes," he said, "they're strict about matters of decency. And did you notice how carefully they washed themselves?"

"Yes. And they washed their pants too."

"They do it every time. That means at least once a day."

We went indoors to tidy the place up, as the young couple would be coming presently to dress for the *funcia*. We had soon put things straight, and I sat down on a tree stump outside.

Pacchilla stretched before me—a collection of *palma brava* huts straggling up the hillside. This place had once been a clearing in the forest colonized by an overflow of population from Lamas, for the surnames here were all Lamas names—Tapullima, Amasifuen, etc.

"Come on, Bernardo. It's time to go to the bridegroom's mother."

"I'm ready."

When we got there, the Indians standing around looked at me and then spoke in Quechua.

"You've done very well to go barefoot," Arquimedes explained.

"Your prestige is soaring. In their hearts, you know, they despise people who wear boots or shoes. What they're saying about you is that you're the first half-caste they've ever seen walking about like them."

The scene round the house was unforgettable. To leave the interior free, the cooking was being done outside. On huge wood fires a gargantuan meal was simmering in gigantic *cantaros*. Ninety guests were invited. In one *cantaro* alone forty chickens in very little water were being reduced to a soup. I was offered a bowl of it then and there. This *caldo*, as it was called, could have held its own against the products of the finest chefs in France. I felt as if I had been whisked back four centuries to the days of the good King Henry of Navarre.

I had hardly done scalding my lips when the mother of Cristobal Tapullima, the bridegroom, called me in to breakfast. The feast was beginning that was to last all day. Sucking-pig *sauté* and various other meats were followed by cakes and coffee. Then, after a brief respite, came *chicha* and *aguardiente*. The *chicha* was excellent. Five enormous jars of it had been made specially, and each jar held well over twenty gallons. It was poured out into a calabash and passed round, each one drinking just as much as he liked.

Presently thirsts seemed to be more or less slaked, though it may well have been that the guests were simply holding back for something more important that was to follow.

"What a time they are taking to get dressed!" said a young Indian, whom I had been watching as he painted his face.

"Do you often paint your face?"

"Almost every day."

Others were doing the same—in fact, practically all the young men —the colour used being a brilliant red. As for the patterns, there was a choice of only three (*see sketch*).

"Where do you get that red from?"

"From a plant called *achote*."

It was in liquid form and was daubed on with a finger.

One of Cristobal's young brothers, sent off to scout, came back saying the bridal pair were ready to be fetched. A cry of joy went up all round:

"Ah! *Haya!*"

Cristobal's mother—astonishingly young for her forty years— turned to Arquimedes. For it was he who had to give the signal. When he did, we all marched off to the *padrino's* house, led by a band.

The band consisted of three, whose instruments were the *pifano*, *bombo*, and *redoblante*. The *pifano* is a sort of flute, with five holes in front and one behind. The opening at the top has a U-shaped notch which is held just under the lower lip, the upper lip protruding slightly. The *bombo* is a bass drum with a snare drawn tightly across the under side. The *redoblante* is a shallow side-drum.

The young couple kept us waiting a few minutes longer. Then they came out, to be greeted by joyful acclamation.

The bride, a girl of fifteen, had a copper-coloured skin of exquisite freshness. She was absolutely serene, her features betraying nothing. The bridegroom, Cristobal Tapullima, couldn't have been much older, and his face too was impassive.

The bride wore a gathered skirt, cyclamen in colour and embroidered, and a white blouse. Her shoulders were covered by a large silk shawl, her head by a kerchief, knotted behind, so big that the ends fell to her waist. Wearing an enamel crown adorned with gold beads and multicoloured tin foil, she looked like a young queen. She wore large earrings and lots of necklaces and bracelets. She was sheltered by an umbrella from the sun.

The bridegroom was all in white.

They moved off towards the young man's house, and the rest of us followed behind, in no particular order, forming an unrehearsed procession.

The band led the way, the drums beating wildly. The *funcia* was now in full swing.

When still a hundred yards from Cristobal's house, shots were fired by young Indians with painted faces.

"They're to frighten away any evil spirits that may be lurking in the young people's bodies," Arquimedes explained.

We reached the house where the *cantaros* were still simmering away on their wood fires, giving off alluring smells.

Except for those of the bridal pair, all faces were wreathed in smiles, mine no less than the others, for the gaiety was infectious.

It was some time before the guests entered the house. We waited outside on the reddish terrace of beaten earth, chatting, laughing. Only a stone's-throw away was the impenetrable forest.

"Come," said Arquimedes. "I have the honour of being the first guest to cross the threshold."

I went in behind him and others followed. Arquimedes and I sat down at a little table with the bridegroom. Other men squatted on the floor all round the room. Facing us was a similar table at which the bride sat with Arquimedes' wife, her godmother. On each table stood a bottle of *aguardiente* and a pitcher of *chicha*.

We settled down in something like silence. Then Arquimedes made a sign to the musicians, who were against the wall opposite the door, and they struck up at once an air on the *pifano* accompanied by the brisk rhythm of the *bombo* and *redoblante*.

"This is the first dance, the *cumplimiento*."

So saying, Arquimedes squeezed past me and took up his position in the space which had been kept clear in the middle of the room.

One after the other, he called up his wife, the bridegroom's mother, and then the bride's father, who formed up and started a sort of quadrille. With an arm raised and slightly bent, each waved a handkerchief during the different figures of the dance, the men fanning their partners' faces.

Meanwhile women were going round distributing *biscuchuelos*, cakes made of maize, sugar, and yolk of egg. *Chicha* and *aguardiente* were poured out freely. Only the bridal couple neither ate nor drank. They sat absolutely still, their eyes lowered, the right hand resting on the left. Except for one dance, in which they took part, they were to stay like that till one in the afternoon.

In that dance two quadrilles formed up simultaneously. In one were the bride and bridegroom and their godparents, in the other the parents.

This dance, the *marinera*, was very like the *cumplimiento*, except for an interruption in the middle, when a friend came forward with *biscuchuelo* crumbs and a bottle of *aguardiente*. Scattering the crumbs over the heads of the dancers, she then spattered them freely with the brandy, which trickled down their faces, wetted their hair and clothes and even got into their eyes. Strongly alcoholic, it of course evaporated at once.

The dancers started again, bearing the stinging of their eyes with fortitude, for it would have been bad form to make a fuss.

Only when he resumed his seat next me did Arquimedes wipe his eyes. The bridal couple sat down too, resuming their expressionless attitude.

I asked Arquimedes the meaning of it.

"They mustn't eat, they mustn't drink, they mustn't talk, they mustn't move. It's an ancient custom coming down from the religion of their ancestors. If they did they'd spoil the future for themselves and their children. Their crops would fail."

From this time onwards everyone could dance. Another dance, much wilder than the *marinera*, was the *raspa*, quite a savage affair, only remotely resembling the dance we know by that name.

Frenzy mounted steadily. The strongly rhythmic music worked its way into one's very bones, and the floor of beaten earth throbbed with it. The musicians seemed to be in ecstasy, their eyes lost to all around them. The *pifano*-player blew for all he was worth the whole time, while the man on the *redoblante* beat sometimes on the head of his drum, sometimes on the cylinder, producing the most subtle rhythms.

Occasionally between the dances a young man played a melancholy tune on the pipe that was slung from his shoulder on a beautifully embroidered band. Everyone knew what it meant—that he was in love with one of the girls present—and they tried to guess who it might be.

Each dance lasted a long time, as I knew only too well, since I had to dance myself. The Indians, completely won over by my bare feet, insisted on my taking part in everything. My beard too contributed to my success. The Lamistas have hairless faces and were fascinated by my growth, coming up to me to touch it and even to give it a pull to make sure it was genuine.

If the dances were wild, they were extremely chaste. A man hardly so much as touched his partner, and few words were exchanged. It may also be said here that the Lamistas have a strict and very exalted conception of love. Adultery is exceedingly rare, and it is practically unthinkable for an engaged couple to have pre-nuptial relations.

At one o'clock, when Arquimedes gave the signal for the dancing to stop, I wasn't sorry, being pretty well exhausted. A big table was set up in the middle of the room and the guests sat down to the feast. Even now the young couple ate nothing. They were served like everyone else, but put their helpings into a special *cantaro* called an *alceo*, the word meaning literally 'keep for later'.

When the meal was over, Arquimedes' wife stood up and recited some prayers for the dead of the family. Only then were the young couple free to retire to a room where they could be alone—failing that, to the forest—and have their first meal together.

What happened next was what happens the world over: the women washed up while the men idled around. I made use of the time myself to inspect an oven built in the same style as the one I had seen by Warachi's house at Cuypa. A square foundation, whose sides were just over thirty inches, was surmounted by a dome in which the bread was cooked. Another ancient Inca tradition to which these far-flung offspring had remained faithful.

Arquimedes joined me and we drank some *aguardiente* together out of a calabash, toasting the newly married couple. In another hour we should be going up to the bride's house. Her mother went home now to get ready to receive us.

Arquimedes wandered off. A young Indian came up to me.

He limped, having a festering sore on his big toe at the base of the nail. Anxious as I was to worm my way into their lives as much as possible, I seized on the opportunity offered.

"Would you like me to treat it for you?"

"If you like."

"Then fetch me a clean rag, some soap, and some *aguardiente*."

He did as he was bid, and I took him aside. I began by washing the rag, which was more grey than white, with *aguardiente*. After leaving it a minute or two to dry, I tore it in two, and used one half to wash the wound, first with soap and water, then with *aguardiente*. He made

N

quite a fuss as the latter stung him, but I twitted him, telling him to be a man.

He made no answer to that, but he stopped groaning, gripping a branch instead.

I washed the place once again, then bandaged it up with the bit of rag I had kept in reserve, though I knew very well the dressing wouldn't stay in place more than five minutes if he walked about.

The real point of this story is that I was promptly dubbed a sorcerer, a reputation which soon gained strength when it transpired that I knew a thing or two about their native magic. This was useful, as it helped to break down their reticence on this subject.

A woman brought a small child to me on whose left arm was a bracelet made of a few seeds on a cotton thread.

"What are these seeds?" I asked.

Picking them out one by one, the Indians named them.

"This one's called *llantero*, this one's *sinchi kaspi*, this one's *inayuca*. . . ."

"And what's it for?"

"It protects the child against illnesses and spells."

I thought this a favourable moment to inquire once again about the iguana bracelets worn by the adults.

"And this one?" I asked, taking hold of an Indian by the wrist.

A brief silence, then:

"If you put an iguana bracelet on any limb it makes it strong."

I'd waited a long time for that!

As we talked I was eyeing four Indians whose left arms were tattooed. It is apt at any time to be a delicate matter to inquire into the reasons for a man's being tattooed, and with primitive peoples one does not know what sacred or magic meanings may not reside in it.

I therefore approached the subject gingerly. In the end my diplomacy was at least partially rewarded. Of the four patterns illustrated, A and B (the latter on the arm of a man of sixty) represent a creature called *alacran*, a sort of scorpion haunting the forests, and serve to keep the tattooed man from the justly dreaded sting. C represents the sun, so important in the mythology of the Incas, since it is their god.

The Indian wearing pattern D was a much tougher customer. He tried to fob me off with the usual evasion that it was a decoration—to 'make pretty' as he put it. And when I returned to the attack he took refuge in laughter.

I pretended to take no further interest, handed round a calabash of *aguardiente*, and talked of other things.

Then suddenly with a smile:

"And that tattoo mark?" I asked.

He smiled back.

"Do you really want to know?"

"Of course I do. And the others have told me about theirs."

That seemed to get home. There was a long council of war at the end of which he seemed to have made up his mind to tell me. As

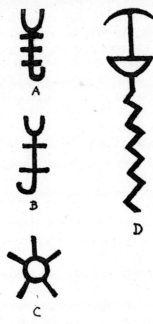

Arquimedes was to tell me later, it was really my bare feet which helped more than anything.

The top part of pattern D is an anchor, the zigzag line below being lightning or, alternatively, rain. As for the magical property of the symbol, all I could get out of him was that it was to "hold up the boat's anchor", which meant all the less to me when I reflected that these people here were not even *balseros*.

After this lull in the *funcia*, Arquimedes formed us up into a procession, which, headed by the band, climbed up the steep path through a corner of the forest to the house of the bride's parents.

All was lightness and gaiety. Under the influence of the rhythmic music, these graceful bodies moved with the beauty of a ballet. The young men's painted faces and sky-blue shirts, the long dark-blue skirts of the women, the waving handkerchiefs, the piercing notes of the *pifano*—all combined to make an unforgettable impression on me.

The bride's parents were on the threshold to greet us. The procession broke up: some went indoors, others stayed outside. Talk was resumed, everyone drank. Green oranges were handed round, oranges such as are unknown in Europe. Though green they were absolutely ripe, deliciously sweet and juicy. Many took the opportunity to have a *siesta*. For my part, I lay down on the grass under a scented lemon tree and had a little nap. The sexes appeared quite spontaneously to have separated. All the men on one side of the house, all the women on the other. The ages had sorted themselves out too. It was the young men who slept while their elders went on talking and passing round little calabashes of *aguardiente*.

It was the bride's younger sister who woke me up with a laugh and a handful of oranges. I nudged my neighbours and getting out my knife 'good for killing man', I peeled the oranges and divided them up. I explained to them that my knife's nickname had been given it by an Indian of the Beni. I even wrote it on the sheath with my ball-point pen. More admiration!

"He knows how to write!" they said.

The brides's sister came back to call me into the house.

"You're wanted."

Going indoors out of the bright sunshine into the dark interior I could at first hardly see a thing. But Arquimedes called me and, moving in the direction of his voice, I soon made out a group of people sitting in a corner.

"*Amiguito*," said the bride's father, "will you have some *aguardiente* with us?"

He held out a calabash he had just filled. I took a sip, then passed it on to Arquimedes. No: that wouldn't do! I must take a proper draught or my host would be offended.

I stayed there a quarter of an hour. Then Arquimedes said it was time to be going down, as the dancing would be starting again.

I left that house a little sadly. It was the only restful place I had found that day. The afternoon was drawing in when we all straggled back to the bridegroom's house.

I noticed that not only the two families concerned but a large number of the guests called Arquimedes *compadre*. He had acted as *padrino* at so many marriages that the title was appropriate.

"You see, *cholito*," he explained, and when he called me *cholito*, little half-caste, I glowed with pleasure, "you see, I have to pay for the musicians and it's I who have to dress the bride and bridegroom. It costs quite a lot of money. But I can't grumble: I never have to buy any firewood or any bananas, my *compadres* bringing me all I want. And if my house is in need of repair they see to it."

The dancing had been in full swing for some time.

Each Indian had now a bottle of *aguardiente* slung from his shoulder on a narrow hand-woven white band embroidered with patterns in red and blue. Those who heard Arquimedes call me *cholito* followed suit, even those who didn't speak Spanish.

"*Cholito*," they would say, coming up to me and handing me their bottle or a little calabash of *aguardiente*.

The *chicha* was flowing freely too, the women constantly going off for fresh supplies from the *depositos*. Each time, they came to offer me some, till I was a little embarrassed by my importance.

The dancing, which was supposed to last till nightfall, in fact went on till midnight. Then at last Arquimedes gave the signal for it to end. The musicians played a little piece, the *sitaracuy*, which provided a transition between the frenzy of the *funcia* and the long silence of the night.

The guests drifted off to their homes, leaving just a handful of us—the parents of the young couple, Arquimedes, his wife, and me to accompany Cristobal and his young wife to the new house which awaited them a little to one side of the village. This last little ceremony was the *pañucho*—'the going to sleep'.

. . . . .

I woke at dawn.

"Are you coming for a wash?" asked Arquimedes.

We went down together to the little artificial waterfall under which my friend's son was splashing about and laughing with half a dozen little Indian boys.

"Make haste, *cholito*. We've got to go to a *consejo*."

I asked what the council was about.

"I'd rather you saw for yourself. If there's anything you don't understand, give me a nudge and I'll explain it to you. Only, don't insist. If I can't tell you then, we'll have plenty of time on the way home."

Washing over, we went straight to the house of Cristobal's parents. Properly speaking, the meeting ought to have been in the *padrino's*, but the house that had been lent to Arquimedes was too small to hold all the guests.

In front of the house, Cristobal's mother welcomed me with a broad smile. We went in, and Arquimedes sat down on a bench in the middle of the opposite wall. His wife sat on his right, with Cristobal's parents next to her, I on his left. The bride's parents sat against the wall facing us. The remainder stowed themselves away as best as they could, sitting or standing.

In front of us, just a few feet away, two stools had been placed, and on these the bride and bridegroom took their places. They were dressed as on the previous day, except that the bride wore no ornaments.

In a religious silence, Arquimedes began to speak, addressing Cristobal in these words:

"Today you are no longer a child, but a man, and there are certain things you must know. I am your *compadre*. By your side is your wife: you must love her and help her and protect her and see she has all she needs. You must not raise your hand against her, and, when she wants to see her parents, you must let her go. For if she is your wife, she is still their daughter. It is they who have brought her up. Now that you are married, you belong to her family too: they are also your parents and whatever they want of you that must you give. If they want logs to burn, you will cut wood for them in the forest and bring them enough. When you go shooting you must think of them and give them their share.

"Neither must you forget your own parents, for it is them you must thank for being what you are today, a man. When you were little, they gave you all you needed to grow up. One day you will have children too, and you will owe them as much as you owe your parents today. Neither must they go in want.

"Do you understand me?"

Almost too moved for speech, the young man nodded and the faintest "*si*" came as a whisper from his lips. Arquimedes then turned to the girl.

"Did you hear what I said to your husband?"

Still more moved, and furtively wiping away a tear, the bride nodded. The *padrino* continued:

"Your husband who is by your side. . . . You must look after him, cook for him, sew for him, mend for him, wash for him. You must also keep your house clean. But above all you must obey your husband and follow him everywhere. When he goes out to his *chacra*, you will go with him and help him in all the work on the land. When you have children, you shall take care of them and feed them well, as your mother did for you. You must also be good to your husband's parents, giving them all the help they ask."

It was then the godmother's turn, and Arquimedes' wife repeated what he had said. Everybody was touched. Many of the women wept; the men looked grave. I was conscious that this was a moment of supreme importance, far from being a mere formality.

Next, Arquimedes called on Cristobal's parents to speak, and after them came the bride's. They all said the same thing.

So far we had heard of nothing but virtues. It was now time to deal with the failings, the two families exchanging reproaches concerning their son-in-law or daughter-in-law. It was the bride's father who began:

"Cristobal, you're often lazy when there's work to do in the fields. How do you expect to be able to feed my daughter?"

Cristobal hung his head, saying nothing.

"From now on," put in Arquimedes, "he will be working not only for himself but for the woman he loves. Love gives good heart. Never forget that you're a man now."

"Last year he told a lie during the feast of Santa Maria at Lamas when he wanted to go gadding about with the other boys of his age."

"It's a very grievous thing to lie, but last year he was still a child. One can't expect anyone to be perfect, least of all a child."

A grateful look from Cristobal.

His mother took up the tale.

"Of course my son isn't perfect, but your daughter is a chatterbox. How often have I not heard her yapping with other girls at the fountain. But then of course a wagging tongue is a family failing. . . ."

The sparks would soon have been flying had not Arquimedes cut her short. He was an old hand at this job. Turning to me, he said:

"One always has to be careful the *consejo* doesn't degenerate into a brawl. It sometimes happens, though very rarely, that the two families come to blows. I think it's such a shame that a beautiful wedding should end in anger. So I always try to keep a nice family atmosphere."

A few more criticisms were hurled at the young people's heads, but Arquimedes saw to it that no damage was done, and at the end the families were on as good terms as ever.

The young people then came and knelt before everyone in turn to receive a blessing or some good advice. When Cristobal knelt in front of me, he put his right hand on my knee. I put mine on his shoulder and wished him happiness and prosperity.

With that the wedding celebrations were over. Life would now resume its normal course. From its moment of jubilation, Pacchilla would now return to sober reality. The *chacras* would soon be full of men and women tending their cotton or their bananas.

A young Lamista came forward with the mule for Arquimedes' wife. She mounted, and we all went off together. Before plunging into the forest, we turned round. Our hosts were waving to us, Cristobal and his young wife smiling.

We went back by a slightly different route, as Arquimedes' wife wanted to look at a *chacra* which belonged to them.

We had been walking a little more than an hour when it began to rain—heavy tropical rain which trickled down from the leaves of the gigantic trees around us. In no time we were wet through.

"This is what the Indians do when it rains," said Arquimedes, peeling off his shirt. "You'd better do the same."

He took off his trousers too, keeping only his underpants. His small son, who had run on ahead, came back. He hadn't waited to be told. I promptly imitated them. Our wet clothes were rolled up in a bundle and on we went. The boy was extraordinary. Running ahead, then coming back to us, he covered far more distance than we did, yet he was tireless.

Suddenly the forest disgorged us and we found ourselves looking down on a wide stretch of country, a valley as green as any in Normandy, at the bottom of which ran a little *rio*. Two isolated houses looked absurdly small.

We started down the steep side of the valley. Arquimedes' wife, afraid the mule might slip on the wet grass, got down and walked. I carried the little girl, perched up on my shoulders. The rain stopped and we halted by the river to put our clothes on again.

On the opposite slope the forest began again. Long streaks of mist hung about the tree-tops. The hot earth was steaming, making the atmosphere like that of a hot-house.

The rain had also brought out all the smells—that of the humus and of the grass, while heady whiffs, redolent of oriental luxury, floated to us from some aromatic tree.

In the heat of the sun our clothes were soon dry again. In a quarter of an hour we reached the *chacra*.

"*Su casa*," said Arquimedes' wife. "You're at home."

We stopped for a while. A young half-caste emerged from a hut bringing us fruit and a calabash of *aguardiente*. The other house was a distillery. Arquimedes explained the process to me; it was a very primitive one. A large heap of wood ash had already told me what fuel they used.

Some sacks full of a dark wet substance were dripping into an earthenware basin.

"What's in those bags," I asked.

"Ash. They're extracting the potash from it. They kill two birds with one stone here, using the by-product to make soap."

"But they need fat for that. What do they use?"

"Lard or brazil-nut oil. Of course all the best nuts are sold as such. But any mouldy ones are used for soap-making."

"We know something about soap-making in France. During the war, many people had to make their own. With tallow. That was the only fatty substance we could get."

Arquimedes and his wife stared at me in amazement. War-time privations are difficult to imagine in a country where nothing is lacking. I told them something about those dark years from 1940 to 1945.

"It's awful!" they cried. "You went in daily fear of air raids and had nothing to eat! And to think that we here had everything, even soap! All the same, there is nothing we could have done for you, however much we tried."

We had to be getting on, so as not to arrive too late at Lamas. After less than ten minutes' walk the rain began again, and now among the *chacras* we hadn't even the partial shelter of the trees. Once more we took our clothes off. That gave us freer movement, but even so the pace was slow, as the sodden ground was heavy going. Arquimedes' wife, riding once again, kept as dry as she could under the umbrella that had served as the bride's sunshade the previous day.

I had never been under such a deluge—fortunately a warm one,

It came down absolutely steadily, relentlessly, rushing in little torrents down the hillside.

Hours passed.

When at last we neared Lamas, Arquimedes said:

"We can't go into the town like this. Pouring though it still is, we've got to put our clothes on. We haven't much farther to go now."

We struggled into our wet clothes, and trudged on, slipping at every step. I was never more glad to get indoors than when we finally passed through Arquimedes' doorway.

Though I knew I would be staying a few days more at Lamas to tie up, with the help of my many friends in the quarters of Sangamas and Shupinghuas, some of the loose ends in what Jean-Luc and I regard as no more than a preliminary canter in ethnological research, it was that evening that I was to say good-bye to Arquimedes.

The Lamista marriage which, thanks to him, I had been privileged to witness had brought me far closer to the Indians than I had ever been before. The beauty of that ceremony and the simplicity and sincerity of all who took part in it had touched me profoundly.

"Arquimedes, how can I ever thank you?"

"Don't try, *cholito*. It will only make our parting the sadder," he answered.

With a silent handshake, I left him, and walked through the streets alone. The rain had stopped. The Indians I met passed me with a friendly greeting. I was no longer a stranger. I had come to study their lives and they had taken me into them.

Warachi, Aramayo, Jean-Luc, the Macho, Cristobal Tapullima and his family, Arquimedes—I thought of them all that evening and of many others, men who were united in the simple word 'friendship', and who differed in nothing but the customs they observed.

INDEX